D1606274

THE
HISPANIC-AMERICAN
ENTREPRENEUR

An Oral History of the American Dream

TWAYNE'S
ORAL HISTORY SERIES

Donald A. Ritchie, Series Editor

BEATRICE RODRIGUEZ OWSLEY

THE
HISPANIC-AMERICAN
ENTREPRENEUR

An Oral History of the American Dream

TWAYNE PUBLISHERS · NEW YORK
Maxwell Macmillan Canada • Toronto
Maxwell Macmillan International • New York   Oxford   Singapore   Sydney

Twayne's Oral History Series No. 8

The Hispanic-American Entrepreneur: An Oral History of the American Dream
Beatrice Rodriguez Owsley

Copyright © 1992 by Twayne Publishers

Twayne Publishers
Macmillan Publishing Company
866 Third Avenue
New York, New York 10022

Maxwell Macmillan Canada, Inc.
1200 Eglinton Avenue East
Suite 200
Don Mills, Ontario M3C 3N1

Macmillan Publishing Company is part of the Maxwell Communication Group of Companies.

Library of Congress Cataloging-in-Publication Data

Owsley, Beatrice Rodriguez.
    The Hispanic-American entrepreneur : an oral history of the
American dream / Beatrice Rodriguez Owsley.
        p.   cm.—(Twayne's oral history series ; no. 8)
    Includes bibliographical references and index.
    ISBN 0-8057-9107-8—ISBN 0-8057-9115-9 (pbk.)
    1. Hispanic Americans in business—Louisiana—New Orleans
Metropolitan Area—Interviews.   I. Title.   II. Series.
HC107.L82N46   1992
338'.04'08968073—dc20   92-9230
                                                                              CIP

The paper used in this publication meets the minimum requirements of American National Standard for Information Sciences—Permanence of Paper for Printed Library Materials. ANSI Z3948-1984. ∞™

10 9 8 7 6 5 4 3 2 1 (hc)
10 9 8 7 6 5 4 3 2 1 (pb)

Printed in the United States of America

To Jim, Judy,
and the Three Amigos

Contents

Foreword

The debate over multicultural influences in American life raises significant questions about the Hispanic-American community. Should Spanish-speaking or Spanish-surnamed Americans be identified as Hispanic-American, or is this simply a convenient, "Eurocentric" census term that clusters together people of diverse nationalities? How have Hispanic-American communities formed within Anglo-America, and what features hold them together and differentiate them from those around them? Does their experience suggest that American society remains a "melting pot," or have their separate cultural identities resisted assimilation? Can the United States be one people out of many, or have we become a disunited nation? By using oral history to examine the Hispanic-American entrepreneurs of New Orleans, Beatrice Rodriguez Owsley offers new responses to these questions, in the words of those who are actively pursuing the American dream. And despite the varieties in their backgrounds, these narrators express a common triumph of ambition over alienation and a strong sense of purpose for themselves, their families, and their community.

Oral history may well be the twentieth century's substitute for the written memoir. In exchange for the immediacy of diaries or correspondence, the retrospective interview offers a dialogue between the participant and the informed interviewer. Having prepared sufficient preliminary research, interviewers can direct the discussion into areas long since "forgotten," or no longer considered of consequence. "I haven't thought about that in years" is a common response, uttered just before an interviewee commences with a surprisingly detailed description of some past incident. The quality of the interview, its candidness and depth, generally will depend as much on the interviewer as the interviewee, and the confidence and rapport between the two adds a special dimension to the spoken memoir.

Interviewers represent a variety of disciplines and work either as part of a collective effort or individually. Regardless of their different interests or the variety of their subjects, all interviewers share a common imperative: to collect memories while they are still available. Most oral historians feel an additional responsibility to make their interviews accessible for use beyond their own research needs. Still, important collections of vital, vibrant interviews lie scattered in archives throughout every state, undiscovered or simply not used.

Twayne's Oral History Series seeks to identify those resources and to publish selections of the best materials. The series lets people speak for themselves, from their own unique perspectives on people, places, and events. But to be more than a babble of voices, each volume organizes its interviews around particular situations and events and ties them together with interpretive essays that place individuals into the larger historical context. The styles and format of individual volumes vary with the material from which they are drawn, demonstrating again the diversity of oral history and its methodology.

Whenever oral historians gather in conference, they enjoy retelling experiences about inspiring individuals they met, unexpected information they elicited, and unforgettable reminiscences that would otherwise have never been recorded. The result invariably reminds listeners of others who deserve to be interviewed, provides them with models of interviewing techniques, and inspires them to make their own contribution to the field. I trust that the oral historians in this series, as interviewers, editors, and interpreters, will have a similar effect on their readers.

DONALD A. RITCHIE
Series Editor, Senate Historical Office

Acknowledgments

As a trained archivist and a Hispanic, I felt compelled to record the story of the contemporary Hispanic community in New Orleans, and so in 1985 I began an ongoing oral history project on the group. The oral history interviews used in this book, along with others generated from the project, are available at the University of New Orleans. I owe a special debt to the narrators who participated in the project and regret that not all the stories could be included herein, inasmuch as each narration shares equal importance in presenting an accurate picture of the community. I am also greatly indebted to D. Clive Hardy, archivist at the university, for his support in this endeavor.

The nine newspaper articles in appendix 2 were originally published in and are reprinted here with the permission of the New Orleans *Times-Picayune*. I am grateful to Jim Amoss, the paper's editor, for his assistance.

Last, I want to thank my husband, Jim Owsley, for his useful comments, patience, and encouragement.

Preface

As the daughter of Colombian immigrants, I grew up in New York City during the 1930s. Although family friends included Anglo-Americans, for the most part they originated from various Spanish-speaking countries and had come to the United States for economic, personal, or political reasons. Together we frequented social gatherings (sponsored by a local Catholic church) where Latin American poetry, music, and dances were performed and dined in restaurants where Mexican and Spanish delicacies were served. Consequently, at an early age I was acquainted with the vibrant sounds and colorful sights indigenous to Spanish-American cultures.[1] Forty years later, demographic changes in New Orleans, Louisiana, generated a Hispanic community with amenities similar to those I had enjoyed as a child in New York.[2] In like manner, the new immigrants differed in race, economic standing, and education but were united by heritage and language. The presence of a large and growing Hispanic community resulting from economic and political turmoil in Latin America had by 1980 become an emerging reality, and its importance in New Orleans became apparent to even the casual observer.

Similar occurrences took place in other cities throughout the United States. To assess the new migration, the U.S. Department of Commerce included the designation "Spanish/Hispanic Origin" in its 1980 census and printed its questionnaire in both English and Spanish.[3] Newspaper and television coverage spoke of this phenomenon, and monographs devoted to immigrants from a particular country were published regularly.[4] Nevertheless, a need existed to document social and economic conditions within the entire community and to explore how the growing number of immigrants interacted with one another. In 1985 I began an ongoing project at the University of New Orleans to examine these issues as they concerned members of the local Hispanic community. To carry out the investigation I chose the methodology of oral history, since prior ethnic studies using this approach had yielded rich testimony.[5] This book on Hispanic-American entrepreneurs is based on a segment of that project.

A questionnaire was drawn up to gather information on family background, social and economic standing in the community, perceptions on American and Latin American cultures, and problems encountered on arrival in the new environment. Although initially clergy, social workers, and local civic leaders provided lists of potential interviewees, once the project commenced I received numerous referrals of persons eager to participate. Introductory letters outlining the project were sent to prospective narrators, and follow-up telephone calls were made to schedule interviews. To date, 105 persons have been interviewed, 55 of them women and 42 of them men, together representing 16 Hispanic countries as well as Belize (the remaining 8 interviewees represent American-born men and women actively involved in providing local social services to the Latin American community). Their ages at the time of the interviews ranged from 22 to 95, and their levels of education varied from four years of grammar school to graduate-level university credentials. Time of residence in the city similarly covered a wide span, with some having arrived as recently as two years previously and others having been here for as long as 65 years. (A facsimile of the questionnaire and a list of the narrators can be found in Appendix 1.)

Interviews varied in length from 30 minutes to three hours. Many were conducted in Spanish; a few contained discrepancies. The taped recordings were then transcribed verbatim and, when necessary, translated into English. And while transcriptions were later edited to remove false starts and repetitions, care was taken to not alter the content.

The first printed report on Latin American entrepreneurs by the Bureau of the Census appeared in 1969, and subsequent studies on the subject gradually became accessible.[6] A comparison of the reports for 1972 and 1982 showed that the number of Hispanic-owned businesses, had doubled in 10 years and that existing companies were not targeted to one particular market. The 1982 report also ranked Louisiana tenth in the nation in the number of Latino enterprises in the state.[7] The following remarks from one interviewee underscore this dramatic increase: "While I served as executive director of the Louisiana Hispanic Chamber of Commerce, I learned a great deal about the Hispanic community in New Orleans. I was shocked to learn the vast number of businesses owned by [Hispanics]. Originally I thought there might be 300 or 400. Now I suspect there might be as many as 900 or 1,000 businesses located in the metropolitan New Orleans area. They cover a wide spectrum— from a mom-and-pop food store or beauty parlor to a multimillion-dollar business. Most of the businesses are family-owned or have a sole proprietor."[8]

Given that, statistically, the 1982 report showed that most minority-owned businesses were concentrated in the Greater New Orleans area, this project focused on Hispanic narrators who were either self-employed or proprietors of companies located in the city. Some had elegant headquarters and were listed in trade publications; others based their operation at home.[9] Occupations ranged from architects to tortilla manufacturers, and narrators with similar professions were chosen to emphasize variances in personality, nationality, background, or thought.

Because many narrators experienced difficulty in expressing their thoughts in English, the narrations, as well as other passages in this book, are based on the interviews but not presented verbatim. All narrators approved the essays prior to publication, thus ensuring that the accounts accurately reflect their personal opinions.

The essays are grouped into four main sections, according to shared interests or similar skills. Each section opens with a lagniappe—a term frequently used in New Orleans and, adapted from the Spanish *la ñapa,* implying "something extra given for good measure." Each essay, while covering a segment of the Anglo business community, underscores entrepreneurial traits of foresight, tenacity, and individualism. Because the interviews were conducted over five years (1986–91), the date of each meeting is noted so that the reader can place each essay in its appropriate time period. As a whole, these stories will, I hope, provide insight into different cultures and personalities embodied in Hispanic groups and lead to a greater understanding among Hispanics and Anglos in the United States.

I

INTRODUCTION

NEW ORLEANS
A PORTRAIT OF THE RISE OF HISPANIC
ENTREPRENEURS IN THE UNITED STATES

*Every once in a while I would hear people speaking in Spanish and I
would participate in their conversation because I was desperate to speak to
someone in Spanish.*

This poignant remark[1] describes the bewilderment experienced by many
Hispanics who migrated to New Orleans before 1959. While they saw signs
of a Spanish heritage, stemming from the city's historical and commercial ties
with Latin America, they wondered why Spanish was seldom heard in public
places. A brief overview of conditions prevalent during Spain's 30-year rule
in Louisiana should help clarify why certain Spanish influences persisted in
the culture of New Orleans while others ceased to exist.

Louisiana: From Spanish Colony to Statehood

In 1762, when Louis XV ceded Louisiana to his cousin Charles III of
Spain, the area had been under French rule for 80 years. Not surprisingly,
the French colonists were hostile to the idea of Spanish rule and revolted
against the new governor, Don Antonio de Ulloa. In 1769 Charles III sent
General Alejandro O'Reilly to put down the insurrection and establish Spanish rule in the colony. O'Reilly abolished the French Superior Council, which
combined administrative and judicial powers, and substituted a *cabildo*, or
town council, a type of government employed in other Spanish colonies. He
also introduced Spanish law into Louisiana. During his tenure O'Reilly instituted a number of reforms to improve conditions in the colony and to
promote trade so as to stimulate the local economy.

When Spain took possession, Louisiana was a small colony. The first Spanish census, conducted in 1769, showed a total population of 13,538, and

figures for New Orleans indicated 3,190 inhabitants of that city. Although Spain initially embarked on a strong policy of colonization, this policy caused a financial drain on the home country's economy and was soon discontinued. Consequently, not many Spaniards settled in Louisiana. Most of those who did were officials, soldiers, and farmers, along with a number of merchants from Catalonia who were generally regarded by the Creoles as lower-class. Often thrifty and industrious, some of these Catalons were tavern owners who eventually became wealthy from their ventures. Immigrants from Malaga and from the Canary Islands also settled throughout the territory. The latter, referred to today as Isleños, established one of their larger settlements in the marshes to the south of New Orleans; because of its isolation, this community of Isleños intermarried and preserved its heritage and language. In addition, beginning in 1785 more than 2,000 Acadians arrived from France, their transportation financed by the Spanish government. The Acadians settled in the southern sections of Louisiana and worked as farmers, herders, and fishers.

Spanish rule was generally characterized by tolerance and reconciliation with the French settlers. Although Spanish was declared the colony's official language, its use was not enforced among the colonists. In 1772 the Spanish government established the "Spanish School," a free school for boys, but few youths attended—probably because of a lack of interest in education within the frontier environment and an indifference on the part of the largely French population to learn Spanish. Boys of French ancestry, who did receive an education, went abroad to study or attended private schools operated by French émigrés from Santo Domingo. As a result, by the end of Louisiana's territorial period French and Spanish Creoles spoke a modified French combined with Spanish and containing an admixture of African and Indian words.

Because both the French and the Spanish regimes based their operations in New Orleans, the city retained elements from each culture. French and Spanish cuisines and dining customs had much in common, including the drinking of coffee and wine. In addition, both the French and the Spanish relished a social life that included dancing, music, and outdoor celebrations. As economic conditions in the colony improved during the Spanish regime, a wealthy society evolved that demanded cultural amenities associated with its European heritage, as exemplified by the need for portraitists. José de Salazar and Francisco Salazar became the colony's first known portrait painters. Their paintings, dating from 1792 to 1801 or later, can be found today in public and private collections.

One of Francisco Salazar's more notable portraits was of Don Andrés Almonester y Roxas, who provided funds to rebuild St. Louis Cathedral and Charity Hospital after natural disasters demolished them. Almonester was also instrumental in the reconstruction of the Cabildo and Presbytere located in the Place d'Armes (now referred to as Jackson Square). His daughter, Baroness Pontalba, donated large sums of money for the beautification of the square and was responsible for the construction, in 1849–51, of two of the earliest apartment buildings in the United States, the Pontalba Apartments.

During Spanish rule, the appearance of the French Quarter changed drastically, owing to fires in 1788 and 1794 that destroyed virtually all the area's original structures. Determined to prevent the recurrence of such a disaster, Spanish authorities instituted building codes that required the extensive use of tile roofing and brick. Not surprisingly, many of the new buildings featured elements of Spanish architecture—changes that caused one writer to remark that the French Quarter looked more like Castile than France.

Under Spanish rule, the city's population grew from 3,200 to more than 8,000. Good administrators, the Spanish governors instituted many new services in the city and surrounding areas. The names Ulloa, Galvez, Miro, Carondelet, Gayoso, Salcedo, and Casa Calvo on New Orleans streets serve as reminders of the city's Spanish heritage. Both Bernardo de Galvez, who served from 1777 to 1783, and Francois Louis Hector, Baron de Carondelet, who served from 1792 to 1797, made outstanding contributions during their years in office. Galvez assisted the colonists in their struggle for independence by supplying them with arms and ammunition and by capturing from the British such strategic areas as Manchac, Baton Rouge, Natchez, Mobile, and Pensacola. Baron de Carondelet founded the territory's first newspaper, the *Moniteur de la Louisiane,* and provided security for New Orleans by installing 80 streetlights and organizing a small force of night guards called *serenos.* He also initiated the construction of Carondelet Canal to relieve flooding in the city and to facilitate navigation, and guided the port's increased commercial activity that followed enactment of the Treaty of San Lorenzo, negotiated in 1795 between Spain and the United States. Perhaps the most noteworthy achievement of his administration though, was the establishment of a profitable sugar-refining industry through the efforts of Étienne Boré in 1796.

In 1803 Louisiana went from Spanish to French to American control. Some Spaniards left for Cuba and Mexico, while others, who had married into old French families, remained.[2] In 1812, when Louisiana became a state, New Orleans, because of its geographic isolation from the rest of the country, retained much of the rich Mediterranean culture bequeathed from its heritage as a colony of France and Spain, and did not become like other southern cities. Later generations of Latin Americans migrating to New Orleans would recognize elements of this bequest in the city's environment and culture; such awareness can be found in the testimony of the narrators presented in this volume.

Contemporary Louisiana

Those Latin Americans who arrived in New Orleans in the early years of the twentieth century came individually or in single-family units. Records show that these immigrants included nationals from Honduras, Spain, Mexico, Guatemala, Cuba, Nicaragua, Peru, Costa Rica, Puerto Rico, and Colombia.[3] Some were political exiles, as demonstrated in the 1920 census report listing a significant rise in the number of Mexican nationals in Louisiana concurrent with unstable conditions in their homeland.[4] A few were independent women wishing to experience life away from the confines of a male-dominated society.[5] Others were young men and women from wealthy Latin American families who came to be educated at Dominican College and at Tulane and Loyola universities. And still others came in search of economic mobility. By 1940, 2,279 Latin American aliens were registered in the state.

A majority of these early-twentieth-century immigrants came from coastal cities in Central America that also shipped cargo to the port of New Orleans. Frequently they came to the United States on commercial vessels owned by American companies and remained with friends and relatives until they became accustomed to the new surroundings. During these years a few midtown areas of the city held clusters of Honduran families who were not proficient in English and who depended on one another both for support and for information on available social services. Generally, however, Hispanics resided throughout the city; there were no barrios.[6]

The majority worked for Anglo establishments. Department stores carrying higher-priced merchandise hired persons of Spanish origin to assist those wealthy Latin American families who made numerous shopping trips to the city. Some were professionals. Many were clerks in export-import firms. And some were entrepreneurs.[7] Noteworthy among the early merchants was the proprietor of Manuel's Hot Tamales. A Mexican immigrant, Manuel Hernandez was married to a New Orleanian of Italian descent. In 1932 the couple began producing tamales from a recipe that combined Mexican and Creole cooking; Hernandez would sell the tamales at a busy intersection in the city's midtown area for 15¢ a dozen. He then expanded the operation by selling tamales wholesale to vendors, who in turn would sell them throughout the city from pushcarts and station wagons. Manuel's Hot Tamales remains in operation today, with one of Hernandez's daughters as president of the corporation.[8]

While Anglo New Orleanians were almost always friendly and courteous to the immigrant Latin Americans, they were frequently somewhat puzzled as to the geographic locations of the different Spanish countries. "They seemed to think that beyond Mexico the only thing that existed was one big country that was a jungle," said one interviewee.[9] Because the immigrants were not belligerent and posed no threat to the local economy, they encountered no real opposition to their settling in the city.[10]

In 1959, shortly after the government of Fidel Castro took control in Cuba, New Orleans experienced a new phenomenon with the arrival of significant numbers of Cuban political exiles. From 1959 through 1980, these exiles entered in large numbers as a consequence of government and religious resettlement programs. In the beginning the newcomers were from middle- and upper-class families; later many came from the poorer classes.

The first local agency established to serve this Cuban community was the Catholic Cuban Center for Refugee Resettlement, sponsored by the Archdiocese of New Orleans. This agency's services included financial assistance, housing, jobs, and English classes.[11] Residents of Cuban origin formed the Cuban Community Action of Louisiana, a benevolent association that befriended families and assisted with burial arrangements for deceased members and their relatives. Other Spanish-speaking residents worked in programs that sought private donations of furniture, and clothing for the newly arrived. The federal government supplied food stamps, lodging, and monthly subsistence checks for unemployed Cubans.[12] Although 90 percent of the local Hispanics claimed to be Catholic, other religious groups, such as the Baptist Association of Greater New Orleans and the Jehovah's Christian Witnesses, were also active in the resettlement of large numbers of these immigrants.[13]

Unfortunately, passport irregularities, political imprisonment in Cuba, and other difficulties often plagued these Cuban families. Sometimes children traveled to the United States alone to live with friends or relatives. At other times, through sponsorship by the Catholic Charities of New Orleans, children were placed in orphanages and later relocated to foster homes.[14] And on occasion Cuban mothers, fearing future military conscription of their children, fled the country with their young sons. Not all families were reunited, and those who were often had to wait many years for the joyous event, owing to delays caused by the U.S. military blockade of Cuba imposed during the missile crisis of 1962. After travel was restored between Cuba and the United States in 1965, and continuing to 1971, were such families reunited.[15]

Yet Cubans were not the only Latin Americans seeking refuge in the city. During these years, poverty and unstable political conditions in Honduras, Guatemala, Nicaragua, El Salvador, and some South American nations brought many natives of these countries to New Orleans. Consequently, awareness of Hispanic immigrants grew on both the national and local levels. To meet the needs of these immigrants, the federal government increased its annual allocations for public welfare programs, and local chapters of national programs like Service, Employment, and Redevelopment (SER) opened in New Orleans. To assist the ever-growing numbers of Hispanic children who were encountering language difficulties, the Orleans Parish School Board implemented in 22 schools the federally funded program English as a Second Language.

Social interaction within the Hispanic community began to flourish in the 1960s. It started with the celebration of religious services in Spanish and with the formation of numerous social clubs to promote national identity. In the area of mass communication, the first Spanish-speaking radio station was licensed, under the call letters WJMR (later changed to KGLA).[16] Although during the early 1800s New Orleans had enjoyed a wealth of Spanish-language newspapers (records indicated that the first known Spanish publication, *El Misisipi,* started in the city around 1808), during the 1960s such newspapers were not well received.[17] Neither *Siempre* nor *La Prensa,* which began publication in 1967 and 1969, respectively, sustained continued readership, and both were short-lived.

At first, even many individuals with professional education and training took menial jobs; once their language skills improved, however, they quickly found well-paying employment. The new immigrants prompted the U.S. Department of Commerce to issue, in 1969, its first statistical report on minority-owned businesses in the country. The report provided information on firms owned by blacks, Hispanics, and a category designated "Other Minority" that included American Indians and Asians. It noted that 100,000 enterprises in the country were Hispanic-owned, 820 of them located in Louisiana and producing annual gross receipts of $30,559,000. Of the 820 businesses in Louisiana, slightly more than half, or 416, were situated in New Orleans. The report also noted that Hispanic entrepreneurs in the state preferred to be identified under the general heading "Spanish Not Specified." In the main, their businesses were classified as "Retail Trade" and "Service Activities."[18]

During the early 1970s the number of incoming Cubans declined, and by 1975 the ingress finally came to a halt. Immigrants from other Latin American countries, did, however, continue to arrive in large numbers. The 1970 census report listed 70,523 Louisiana residents under the heading "Spanish Origin or Descent."[19] Locally, the Latin American Apostolate was formed in 1972 to eliminate duplicate efforts by various Catholic organizations and lay social workers; it provided a range of special services and sponsored classes in religion and English.[20] By the 1970s Hispanics could be classed in three distinct groups: (a) those who no longer identified with the Hispanic community; (b) those who had assimilated into American culture but still identified with the Hispanic community; and (c) those who were completely disoriented by their new surroundings. Although Hispanics can still be classed in this fashion, it should be noted that, as needs change, individuals may shift from one group to another.[21]

Persons in the first group readily accepted cultural change and participated actively in American society. If they were women and married to American men, their names no longer reflected their Hispanic origin. For example, if "Rosita Sanchez" married "John Woods," her husband would in all probability refer to her as "Rosie" and she become known as "Rosie Woods." Her children might have Anglo names, and generally no effort would be made to teach them Spanish at home. Women in this category who had successful careers usually felt more comfortable in the American milieu because their social and professional dealings were generally with Americans.[22] Even so, such individuals occasionally came to reidentify with their Hispanic heritage.

Persons in the second group consisted mainly of professionals and businesspeople who were comfortable in both cultures and had social contact with Americans as well as Latin Americans. If they owned their own business, they would take advantage of existing minority programs and would apply for available projects offered to minority firms under Federal regulations.[23] Married women in this category made a conscious effort to retain their ethnic identity and often encouraged their children to learn Spanish at home. Conflict arose, however, when mothers, whether married to Spanish or American men, tried to raise their children by adhering only to traditional Spanish values. Torn between the mother's Spanish values and a desire to emulate their American classmates, such children almost invariably rebelled. This struggle gave rise to individuals whose personalities and outlook combined elements of both life-styles.[24]

Persons in the third group were those who encountered considerable difficulty in adjusting to life in the new country. Primarily recently arrived immigrants from rural backgrounds and possessing limited formal education, these persons were overwhelmed by the new culture and its modern technology. Many were illegal aliens fleeing political oppression and living in fear of being apprehended. Others were elderly Hispanics who would or could not learn a new language or make the necessary adjustments to new ideas. Some were housewives who did not speak English and had little contact with people outside their immediate family. And although some members of this group would eventually rise to another category, the group as a whole remained large because of the constant influx of illegal aliens to the city. Individuals from the second group often served as role models for these persons and, through religious and community organizations, brought them out of their isolation and into the mainstream of society.

While social clubs emphasizing national identity continued to flourish in the 1970s, attempts to unite Hispanics as a political force were ineffective owing to a lack of sustained interest in the community.[25] Notwithstanding, a group of Hispanic businesspersons and professionals joined together and created the Greater New Orleans Area Latin American Chamber of Commerce on 10 May 1976. In October of that year the agency became an affiliated committee of The Chamber/New Orleans and the River Region. Hispanic leaders working on the committee planned to strengthen trade between Latin American countries and the port of New Orleans and to acquaint local businesspersons to goods and services available throughout Latin America. Additionally they sought to increase business and professional opportunities for Hispanics in the area.[26]

In this connection, reports on the number of Hispanic entrepreneurs in Louisiana for the years 1972 and 1977, indicated that the largest growth in the state occurred in the metropolitan New Orleans area, where the number of such firms increased from 473 in 1972 to 546 in 1977.

At the same time, figures for the state indicated a decrease in Hispanic-owned companies, from 942 in 1972 to 935 in 1977, but also a rise in their gross earnings, from $44,141,000 to $58,234,000.[27]

In 1980 federal agencies and local charitable organizations again joined forces to resettle the members of another large migration, when the "Freedom Flotilla"—boats manned by private citizens—brought more than 100,000 Cubans to Key West, Florida. Called Marielitos, after the name of the Cuban port of departure, these exiles included some individuals who were mentally or physically ill or had criminal records. Most were young men—differing from earlier Cuban migrants, who mainly had been women, children, and older men.[28] Nor were Cubans alone in this flood of Hispanic immigration. Chaotic political and economic conditions in Central and South America were causing large populations from those areas to seek refuge in the United States. Local church ministries, working through Ecumenical Immigration Services in New York, partly filled the need for providing legal assistance to those Central Americans seeking political asylum.[29]

The 1980 census report listed 99,134 Hispanics residing in Louisiana, 48,415 of them located in metropolitan New Orleans.[30] The ever-growing number of Hispanic residents in the state prompted Governor Edwin Edwards, during his third term in office, to create the post of Assistant to the Governor for Hispanic-American Affairs and in 1984 appointed Esperanza Ferretjans Sciortino to fill this position. At the same time, leaders in the Hispanic community continued their drive to unite Spanish-speaking residents. In 1987, for example, Hispanidad was organized to commemorate Columbus Day, El Dia de la Raza, with a parade and cultural presentations for the general public; its membership constituted representatives from every Latin American business, professional, and social club operating in the city.

Much progress was evident in the area of mass communication. Cervantes Fundación Hispanoamericana de Arte, a nonprofit venture founded in 1980 to showcase Spanish theater, dance, and writers, arranged for a public service television station to videotape many of its programs for mass distribution.[31] Two periodicals in Spanish appeared on the local market. *Que Pasa New Orleans,* begun in 1986, featured timely articles on economic, social, and business events in the city, as well as informative reports on conditions in Latin America.[32] In contrast, *Mensaje,* begun in 1982 by the Department of Hispanic Communications of the Archdiocese of New Orleans, carried articles on religion applicable to the daily life of new immigrants. Funds to support *Mensaje* were raised through an annual Spanish food and music festival that has been well attended by both the Anglo and the Hispanic communities.[33]

Publication of the *1982 Survey of Minority-owned Business Enterprises* enhanced the prestige of local Hispanic entrepreneurs. The survey stated that 2,127 Hispanic-owned businesses with gross sales of $200,810,000 were located in Louisiana and that more than half of these companies, or 1,257, were located in metropolitan New Orleans. Statistically, Louisiana ranked tenth in the nation both in the number of Hispanic-owned enterprises and in the sales and receipts averaged by such firms. In addition, statistical data showed a variance between Louisiana and other states in the breakdown of ownership by country of origin. Figures revealed, for example, that more than 60 percent of Louisiana entrepreneurs were listed under the categories "Other Hispanic," "Other Central or South Americans," and "European Spanish," while less than 40 percent were listed under the categories "Mexican," "Puerto Rican," and "Cuban." This profile was reversed for the remaining states, where ownership of more than 80 percent of the enterprises was designated "Mexican," "Puerto Rican," and "Cuban" and less than 20 percent categorized under the other headings.[34]

While at the time of this writing the official report of the 1990 census is not yet available, estimates for Louisiana show a decrease in the Hispanic population, to about 47,000 in metropolitan New Orleans and 93,044 in the state.[35] A number of factors may have contributed to this change. Lack of available jobs in a area that is slowly recovering from severe economic depression may have persuaded some residents to move to more prosperous locales. Leaders in the Hispanic community have also suggested an undercount in census figures reflecting their group.[36]

According to a U.S. Commerce Department report, in 1987 Louisiana declined to a position of twelfth in the nation in its number of Hispanic-owned companies. Yet the report also showed a growth in the number of local Hispanic firms, listing 2,697 Hispanic businesses with sales of $136,083,000, which 1,719 businesses were located in the Greater New Orleans area, where they produced $86,143,000 in sales receipts.[37] What might account for this increase? For one thing, the 1987 report stated that Hispanic-owned businesses increased across the nation, and in part attributed the increase to a change in IRS regulations giving tax advantages to business firms filing as Subchapter S corporations. This designation allows the ownership of legally incorporated businesses with 35 or fewer shareholders the option of being taxed individually as shareholders rather than as a corporation.[38] For another thing, during the 1980s support groups sponsored in part by the U.S. Small Business Administration were created to assist those Hispanics contemplating new ventures to develop financial strategies for long-term growth. In addition, conferences in Spanish offered by local business-people and universities provided further assistance to the Hispanic business community.[39]

But who are these entrepreneurs? Do they have the same interests and goals as when they arrived as immigrants? And what can we learn from their experiences? The essays that follow may provide some answers and indeed suggest a reevaluation of life in the United States—where, all too often, the native-born tend to take for granted many of the advantages their nation has to offer.

2

THE MARKETPLACE

LAGNIAPPE

While Louisiana was under Spanish rule, currency became more abundant because of the introduction of silver pesos from Mexico. Although consumer goods were produced by local cottage industries, records indicate the existence as well of cotton mills, distilleries, and a small sugar refinery. Local trade was carried on in open-air markets and in a few shops whose inventories indicate that cosmetics, perfumes, fancy soaps, and pomades were much in demand. And while initially most shopkeepers were Spaniards, they were soon replaced by the more aggressive colonists who, along with their descendants, became the major merchants of New Orleans.[1]

AMAURY ALMAGUER

I had occasion to interview President George Bush, governors, mayors, and ambassadors. Although I speak English haltingly, these notables made every effort to understand me. I think they appreciated my desire to succeed.

During our conversation Amaury Almaguer spoke affirmatively of the United States, its people, and its ideology, yet demonstrated nostalgia for Cuba. His manner was tense, not given to flattery, and his answers were succinct—attributable in part to experiences suffered as a Cuban political prisoner. Rather than writing ability, he noted skills in public relations as his greater asset in shaping a journalistic career. He believed that the number of journalists reporting on political events was excessive and preferred writing articles on cultural subjects. In this connection, he pointed to a wall in his office covered with photographs—acquired from prior interviews—of Latin American artists.

In March 1986 Almaguer, along with two associates, published the first issue of Que Pasa New Orleans, *providing a new source of information printed in Spanish. He chose the title to arouse likely buyers' curiosity about local happenings, and the title indeed aptly describes the contents: a reportage covering topics from port activities to sports tournaments. His wife, Imara, assists in writing the copy. Almaguer proudly stated that it was needless to furnish Imara with particulars when asking her to write an article, because they "think along the same lines."[1] His other business interests include a printing company, Lumar Printing Enterprises, and a public relations firm, Hispanic Marketing Associates. Although each company performs a different function, he stated that they share a common goal in going after Hispanic consumers. Almaguer was pleased that Anglos were aware of growing Spanish communities, and each year he calls attention to the accomplishments of local Latin Americans by staging a banquet at which trophies are presented to achievers. In return, he relishes comments classifying the honor as a noteworthy award.[2]*

I was born in Holguín, Oriente Province, Cuba. Mother was a homemaker, and Father was a Cuban soldier. My sister and I attended local schools. I took pleasure in writing, and, while a student, my account of a local sports event appeared in the town newspaper. Life in Cuba was repressive, and if you rejected concepts imposed by the government you were imprisoned. In company with four other youths, I was accused of sabotage for writing messages—conflicting with communistic beliefs—on street walls. Three youths died; two were apprehended. I was sentenced to five years in a penal institution. Although I was 16 years old and prosecuted as an adult, no one tried to secure my release, because I [had] committed a political crime. Actually, Father's behavior suggested that in attacking the Cuban revolution I assaulted him personally. On 4 April 1972 I arrived at Boniato, a prison in Santiago de Cuba, near the city of Guantanamo. Prisoners had the option to enter a rehabilitation program that included work in construction or in sugarcane fields and a reduced sentence, or serve the required period. The latter was severe, in view of the fact that these prisoners received less food, limited medical attention, and had no visitation rights. I chose the harsher sentence. However, if offered the selection today I would again elect prison, with its accompanying physical pain, because my personality evolved from association with inmates who possessed high ideals. I entered prison at 16 and departed at 20 with a tenacious disposition.

On 4 April 1980 over 10,000 Cubans surrounded the Peruvian embassy in Havana, seeking political asylum. On 14 April President James Carter signed an authorization allowing 3,500 Cubans to enter the United States. Other countries participated in the endeavor, and some refugees settled in Canada, Venezuela, and Spain. I was among the political prisoners also released at the time and went abroad to Spain. Spaniards and other Europeans were stirred by the plight of the Marielitos, a name assigned to those émigrés, seeing that they left Cuba by way of the port city of Mariel. I put this interest to my advantage by submitting articles on the event to *Fuerza Nueva,* an ultraconservative Spanish magazine. The editors published the essays after revising my text. As a consequence, my writing skills improved under their guidance.

There were no friends or relatives to greet me when I reached Spain or New Orleans in 1980, but now I have a family. I met my wife, Imara Arrendondo, at a meeting of Tertulia de la Juventud Cubana [a social club for Cuban youth]. The club started as part of a resettlement program to bring new residents, associated with the Mariel flotilla, in contact with Cuban inhabitants in New Orleans. At gatherings we exchanged experiences, discussed Cuban history and political issues. Imara, who came to the United States with her family in 1970, was a club member. We courted for a year, married in 1982, and have a son and daughter.

My first job in New Orleans was with a cement company. I worked as a cementer along the Mississippi River levee. It was fatiguing labor, but I earned money for living expenses. Subsequently the owners of *La Prensa USA*—an American married to a Salvadorian—hired me as photographer, feature writer, and advertising salesman. The newspaper is no longer in operation, but it served as my initial contact with the Spanish business community.

In 1982 a friend employed by the magazine *Replica,* with headquarters in Miami, Florida, called me. He indicated that the editorial staff was searching for a local writer to provide running commentary on New Orleans. I accepted, and later worked in similar fashion for *El Tiempo,* a periodical originating in Honduras, and *USA Entertainment Today.* Supplementary articles have appeared in *Disco Show, Show Continental,* and *Revista Critica,* as well as *El Sol de Haileah,* a Miami-based newspaper.

While working in the marketing department of KGLA, a radio station whose broadcasting is conducted in Spanish, I recognized the need for a magazine in Spanish for those who did not listen to the radio. In truth, there exists a newspaper, *El Mundo Hispano,* published monthly and in operation for 12 years, but it mainly covers topics of international concern rather than local issues. Taking all this into consideration, in March 1986, in company with José Ramón Cosio and César Vásquez, we published the first issue of *Que Pasa New Orleans.* It contained 16 pages; currently the magazine numbers between 40 and 48 pages. Our largest issue was published in January 1989 and totaled 60 pages. It reported on the 30-year exile of many Cubans. Beginning with that issue, we engaged on a policy of developing each issue around one topic. The April publication will focus on Latin American participation in international trade. The May issue, devoted to women, will feature interviews with women and reports of special interest to them. Advertisements, purchased on a yearly basis, appear monthly. In keeping with our new policy, each month we solicit additional ads from companies whose customers would take an interest in our forthcoming topic. To draw a parallel, the issue devoted to women will carry ads from beauty parlors, cosmetic firms, and boutiques. Furthermore, each issue features commentary on art, sports, politics, social events, business, the economy, and a humorous essay. Reporting provides limited but current information on New Orleans.

Ada Cosio, who is married to José Cosio, and I work full-time on the magazine. She serves as bookkeeper, and I gather news, write articles, and sell ads. The others work part-time. José Cosio, the editor, reviews copy and suggests additional features. Imara writes, types copy, prepares layouts and graphics. César Vásquez supervises the monthly printing of 5,500 copies, which normally takes between 9 and 12 days.

Cesar and I own Lumar Printing Enterprise, where the magazine is reproduced. We have a press that generates printed material in Spanish and English. Seventy percent of our trade is with Latin Americans; the balance is with Anglo firms. We create business cards, standardized forms, letterheads, wedding invitations, and birth announcements at competitive prices. We also run off copies of a directory of Hispanic-owned businesses in Louisiana that José Cosio and I compile annually. We began the guide in 1988, compiling the names of advertisers from *Que Pasa New Orleans* and using a format similar to the advertising section of the telephone directory. Initially we printed 20,000 copies of the booklet *Directorio Commercial, Professional y de Servicios de Louisiana* and by 1990 we expect to double this figure.

Recently I opened Hispanic Marketing Associates, a public relations firm that furnishes clients with advertising campaigns directed to Hispanic consumers. We have three important customers: Coors Beer; Our Lady of the Lake Hospital in Baton Rouge, Louisiana; and St. Jude Hospital in Kenner, Louisiana. I prepare an outline of advertising and promotional ideas aimed at stimulating buyer acceptance of a product or service. Imara builds on these concepts and draws up an advertising and marketing program tailored to the needs of the client, and serves as liaison between patrons and our firm.

Although *Que Pasa New Orleans* began as a vehicle to disseminate information on local issues and events, it also contends with difficulties besieging individuals and the region. Our reporting has prompted contributions from readers for those in need of medical assistance, as well as for Casa Nicolas, a nonprofit organization providing food and lodging to homeless youths. We place free advertisements to fledgling businesses and for the unemployed. On occasion we furnish the New Orleans *Times-Picayune* with news stories from Central America when newsmen are not permitted in that locale. At the outset of the prison riot at the facility in Oakdale, Louisiana, in 1987, Salvador Longoria, a lawyer; José Cosio; and I went there to serve as interpreters for the Cuban inmates and contacted the office of Auxiliary Bishop Augustin Roman of Miami, Florida, the cleric who played a pivotal role in pacifying the incident.

I am 31 years old and ambitious. In the future I would like my business interests to grow and prosper. However, I did not come to the United States with the sole purpose of improving my economic status but, rather, to escape the political climate in Cuba. Therefore, if ideological conditions change in Cuba, I will not have a valid reason for remaining here. It will be difficult leaving this country, but at that time I will leave the United States with my family and begin a new venture in my homeland.

T. ARGENTINA AGURCIA

I began working when I was 14 years old, and I am still working, because I am fascinated with my job. Some people say that I am a workaholic.

A "workaholic" can be described as a compulsive worker. In contrast, T. Argentina Agurcia can be characterized as a fortunate individual who discovered her calling early in life and through the years has found it a source of gratification. She is a poised woman, is precise in her conversation, and speaks in clear, dulcet tones. Through her diligent work she has won over many clients who presumed that female accountants were not as competent as their male counterparts. In fact, the accounting firm Suyapa, owned by Agurcia and two other Honduran women, served more than 2,500 customers last year. The firm has its headquarters in New Orleans and a branch office in nearby Kenner, Louisiana.

In addition to her career, Argentina Agurcia enjoys reading books written in Spanish and sharing in family activities. She was born in Honduras and came to New Orleans with her parents, brothers, and sisters in 1957. She and a sister live with their mother, Alba Luz de Agurcia, who is recognized in the community for her efforts to preserve religious traditions indigenous to Honduras. At Christmastime their spacious front room is transformed into a striking nativity setting containing more than 3,500 figurines that were handcrafted in Central America.[1] The pageantry is open to the general public, and newspaper, radio, and television coverage has publicized the event. Another tradition the Mother introduced locally was a yearly celebration on the feast day of the Virgin of Suyapa, the patron saint of Honduras. A statue bearing the image of the saint, along with an altar and kneeling pew made from rich Honduran woods, was donated to St. Teresa of Avila Church, mainly through the fund-raising efforts of Alba Luz de Agurcia. The annual ceremony takes place at the church on 3 February and duplicates, on a lesser scale, the rituals observed in Honduras.

When we met, Argentina Agurcia spoke affectionately about various family members and referred to neighborhoods where they had lived. She wistfully recalled the peaceful life-style she had found in the city in 1957. "I was able to walk freely in the streets," she said. "After work, my sister and I would attend classes to learn English, and we were never fearful of traveling at night. In that respect, New Orleans has changed a lot."

I was born in La Ceiba, Honduras. Originally I had six brothers and two sisters, but two of my brothers died. Mother's ancestry included the notable Acosta family. She married at 17 and was a homemaker. Father worked with

Standard Fruit Company for 45 years, until he became blind from glaucoma. My parents came to New Orleans in search of medical treatment, but, unfortunately, Father was diagnosed as legally blind. However, they were impressed with New Orleans and upon their return encouraged the family to migrate here. In 1957 we came as adults in search of work and looking to improve our economic status. Most of us had studied accounting in Central America. I graduated from the University of Honduras in 1945 with a degree in business.

During the 1950s few persons in the city spoke Spanish. Since I did not speak English, I found employment as a seamstress. At first I took night classes in English; then I studied accounting at Spencer Business College. Later I graduated from Soulé College with a certificate in accounting. My first professional job in New Orleans was with Louisiana Hatcheries. Duties included journal entries, maintenance of cash receipts and cash disbursement journals, preparation of payroll and sales tax returns, posting and balancing the general ledger, and year-end preparation of working papers for independent auditors. I remained with the company for three years. Future employment, with Shushan Brothers Company, from 1960 to 1975, as well as with Pailet and Penedo, where I remained until 1990, involved similar responsibilities.

With family backing, in 1975 I opened a small accounting firm called Agurcia Brothers. For two years I worked full-time trying to expand business. Since profits did not improve dramatically, I found outside employment and continued working evenings and weekends at my firm. Little by little, business grew, and in 1978 two Honduran women who were accountants invested in the firm and we changed the name to Suyapa, in honor of the Virgin of Suyapa. Now business is flourishing, and two of us work full-time, while the third associate continues on a part-time basis. We have not been affected by the sluggish economy in New Orleans, and owners of small businesses in need of accounting services continually contact our firm. Unfortunately, a few customers insist on carrying [on] their business transactions with male accountants. When this situation arises, a brother who manages our branch office will deal with them while we do the work. To date, we have not made a single serious mistake. As humans we have made errors, but only those that were easily corrected and did not pose great problems.

Most of our customers are Hispanic, since we offer the option of speaking in Spanish or English. Many Latin Americans have told us of frustrating experiences in the past whenever they could not communicate their problems to Anglo accountants. By removing the language barrier we can work closely with our clients and advise them on new avenues to save money. However, we always remain within the boundries of the law.

During the time when federal and state income tax forms are filed, we work from 7 in the morning until 10 at night, and many customers come to

21

the office in the evening. We do not make appointments but process clients in the order that they arrive. Year-round, we handle financial records for 27 firms. Three companies are owned by Anglos; the others belong to Hispanics. Our clients are involved in many types of businesses and include travel agents, doctors, lawyers, publishers, exporters, shippers, and retailers.

To properly service our clients, we keep abreast of legislation that leads to changes in federal and state taxes. By the way, I remember how proud I was the first time I learned to process income tax returns. However, to my chagrin, the following year I had to learn an entire new procedure due to changes that evolved from new tax laws. For this reason we attend a minimum of two seminars a year—one on federal taxes and the other devoted to state taxes. They are offered by government agencies as well as private accounting companies and are given in numerous cities. Those sponsored by private agencies may cost as much as $500 for a two-day session. Recently we traveled to Los Angeles to attend a workshop offered by a company whose presentations are excellent.

Over the years, our company has grown through referrals. This year we placed our first classified advertisement. Now that we are well established, we would like to advertise our services on a radio station. I would like to see our company grow to the point where we could employ at least 30 young Hispanics. Not only would they learn proper accounting procedures, but they would be in a position to assist others in the Hispanic community who need assistance in bookkeeping or who require aid in filling [out] an income tax form.

Owning a business can be a satisfying experience. But individuals contemplating this venture should be warned about the many sacrifices that must be made in the beginning. They should never expect an overnight success, but should be ready to devote many hours to ensure its growth. Gradually, the business will expand and problems will become easier to handle.

I would like to continue working at the company for as long as possible. My brother Michael frequently states, "When you do something you enjoy, you will not get tired." I thoroughly agree with his statement. When I return home from a long day at the office, I am never tired, because I am enamored with the field of accounting.[2]

WINSTON HELLING

I accompanied my father on business trips between Guatemala and the United States since I was four years old. Rather than read children's books, I enjoyed listening to his stories on the rise and fall of the Mayan Empire. I was raised differently! Plus, I think what happened was that, from childhood, I learned what money was all about, and it fascinated me.

⁜

Winston Helling began his company in 1980 as a one-man operation selling gaskets to local marine dealerships. Now the firm has dealerships throughout the United States and abroad and employs 30 workers at its headquarters. He believes that employees who are motivated will increase company production and encourages their participation in brainstorming sessions. "I find, in a lot of cases," he says, "that treating people with the respect they deserve and giving them praise for what they are doing go a great deal further than even an increase in pay." He takes stock of new ideas in employee relations, production, and marketing and adapts those which will benefit his operation.

Helling enjoys facing daily challenges in marketing products and participating in the fast-moving business community. Yet he considers inner peace and self-respect paramount over wealth and prestige. His private life centers on his family and membership in the Church of Jesus Christ of Latter Day Saints. During the interview he spoke of his wife as supportive in all his ventures and referred to his father as a positive influence in his life.

My father was born in Philadelphia, Pennsylvania, in 1894. During the greater part of his life, he was a geologist and mining engineer in Central America. He witnessed many political changes in the area and left an unpublished manuscript describing these as well as events in his personal life. In his youth he headed several mining enterprises that were financially successful. Near the end of his life he started a mining company in Guatemala but had difficulties maintaining the firm and eventually lost his capital.

I was born in Guatemala City in 1961. Most people misidentified my father as my grandfather. My mother was born in Guatemala. She had four children from a previous marriage, and I regard them as brothers and sisters. Father spoke several languages and insisted that my younger sister and I learn English and Spanish at an early age. It troubled him that I could not attend the best school in Guatemala, and rather than send me to a school with lower academic standards he had family members teach me to read and write at home. My formal education began when we left the country and came to the

United States. The family settled in New Orleans, and I entered the third grade of school.

As a youngster I collected coins and would spend hours reading literature on numismatics. At 13, I began placing advertisements in the classified section of the daily newspaper and would sell coins to dealers. I was 16 when my father died, and I left school to find employment. A gentleman who was impressed with my business ability in selling him $3 gold pieces told me of a job opening at Kellet Industries, a boat dealer. I went to work in the parts department but was informed that I could sell boats and receive a commission on the sale. Although I was unfamiliar with boat construction, all I knew was that I wanted to make that money. During my first sale I left a customer unattended while I asked a salesman to explain differences between an outboard and an inboard-outboard. As I became knowledgeable, sales increased and in a few years I was earning $20,000 a year. Most employees were only interested in selling big-ticket items, but I also liked working in the parts department. I learned about marine parts and accessories by taking the time to talk to customers who came in to have their motors repaired.

One day the owner's son came upon a catalog from Aqua Power, a company in New York City. Aqua Power was the first firm to compete with engine manufacturers for replacement parts. Included in the catalog was an advertisement for gaskets and O-rings that could serve as replacement parts on Mercruiser motors. At the time, the motor was a popular item on the market but some components were not easily obtainable; consequently, used gaskets were occasionally used to reattach repaired motors to boats. My colleague checked with a rubber manufacturer to see if similar parts could be reproduced locally. It turned out to be a fairly simple procedure, and I was amazed at the disparity in the cost of producing each item compared to its retail price. Upon further investigation, I discovered that we could also purchase components direct from manufacturers who supplied engine builders. I suggested to company officials that we include these items in our parts department, but they did not wish to deviate from the company policy of using only parts supplied by engine manufacturers. Furthermore, the owner informed me that I would have to leave the company if I embarked on the venture. I left and went to work as a salesman for another boat dealership.

In 1979, while vacationing in Florida, I met Cindy, a young lady from Montgomery, Alabama. We shared similar interests and married the following year. We decided to operate a marine-parts dealership from our apartment. With limited funds we started a company called South Central Distributors. We typed a three-page catalog listing 14 components that I knew were used frequently in motor repair and could be obtained locally. I visited a few dealerships and told them we were selling the items listed in the flier at 40 percent below existing wholesale price. Within a few hours I had over $700 in orders. A local rubber manufacturer fabricated dies for the parts and ran off the required quantity. In turn, I processed the orders, and all transactions were conducted by cash-on-delivery. The company became an instant success. To increase sales, I designed an expanded catalog—with illustrations—that was professionally reproduced and mailed to boat dealers around the country. Since our market was no longer targeted to a specific region, we changed our name to Super Gasket. Within three years we were competing with Sierra Supply, a firm affiliated with Equin, a Fortune 500 company.

One day, to my surprise the owner of Aqua Power called me. He wanted to sell the company so he could devote his energy to a new undertaking. I bought the firm and used Aqua Power as our new company name.

Unfortunately, I began to feel invincible, and instead of concentrating on business matters I was caught in the glamour of buying expensive cars and branched out into other fields. I opened a children's furniture and clothing store called Baby Wonderland. Rather than open a small retail outlet, I invested considerably in merchandise. Eventually Aqua Power suffered cash flow problems that led to bankruptcy. In 1984 I had the option to close the company or find investors and continue production. I made a personal commitment that I was going to put the company together again. Bill Monaghan, a former distributor for Mercury Marine, liked our operation and ultimately became our financier. I personally visited most of our creditors and asked for their cooperation during this crucial period. I told them I would supply them with new business for years to come if we could stay in business, but this would require their support.

While finding solutions to problems associated with bankruptcy, I became aware of many changes that had to be made within the company. Over the years, I allowed the company to become an operation where everybody did a bit of everything. For greater efficiency I created separate departments within the firm and assigned specific duties to each worker. I developed in-house facilities to produce our catalogs. I hired two engineers—one to develop new products while the other headed the purchasing department, as he would be sensitive to production needs. But probably one of the best moves that I ever made was to hire a comptroller. He brought a whole different perspective to the company.

Presently transactions are conducted with companies outside of Louisiana. Our current catalog lists over 2,000 motor parts. We are developing 150 new products, but there still remain literally thousands of parts that can be made and sold. Here at Aqua Power we don't want to reinvent the wheel; we just want to take a portion of it, improve it, and bring it to the marketplace with different packaging and pricing.

I have always kept a pad where I write my goals, my ideas, and my accomplishments. I have over 50 goals. Foremost, I want this business to get back on its feet 100 percent. Then I would like to develop some other ideas I have. Eventually I would also like to have my father's manuscript published. Under family goals, I would like to raise our four children in an environment with love. It has been proven that people who write their goals down will have something to shoot for and will accomplish more. We can't go around wandering aimlessly; we have to have some purpose in life.[1]

ROBERT F. DE CASTRO

When I came to the United States, I had limited funds. I sold my horse, saddle, and cows and had to borrow $75 from my brother in order to enter the country with $300. I remember my first winter in New Orleans—it was very cold, and I did not have warm clothing.

Robert de Castro, owner of a thriving enterprise, candidly told me of hardships experienced in New Orleans. Initially, he said, his winter gear consisted of inexpensive woolen underclothes. While these protected him from frigid weather, it was stifling to wear them while working indoors, and the heat would cause his ears to turn bright red. "I was burning, and the heater in the office made it rather uncomfortable for me, but I survived," he remarked. The anecdote underscores de Castro's tenacity.

We met at his headquarters—an elegant facility occupying more than 105,000 square feet—where he employs 55 persons. De Castro started the company more than 38 years ago, when he recognized the need for a local picture-frame importer; previously these items had arrived in the United States through the port of New York. Over the years, the company expanded considerably and it now produces custom-made frames with imported materials arriving through the port of New Orleans. De Castro is friendly and unpretentious, yet his products are sold nationwide and the firm is one of the largest picture-frame-molding distributors in the country. In 1988 the Louisiana Hispanic Chamber of Commerce honored de Castro by naming him "Hispanic Businessman of the Year."

Our meeting took place during Mardi Gras festivities. A local tradition in celebrating Carnival is to catch strings of beads thrown by persons riding parade floats, and a number of these necklaces were on de Castro's desk. He shares the festive mood of Carnival with close associates around the world by enclosing these colorful trinkets in with his business correspondence. He travels several times a year to Europe, the Orient, and Latin America in search of fine woods and superior craftsmanship for his products. As I left his office, he pointed to a large machete hung over an entranceway and said that he had almost severed his leg with a similar instrument while harvesting sugarcane as a youth in Cuba.

I was born on a farm near a small town called Cauto, located in Oriente Province, Cuba. I was one of 11 children; 9 survived, and all but 2 migrated to the United States. My parents were Maria Dolores Fuentes Heredia and Rafael Fernandez de Castro Unruh. They owned a farm where we raised cattle and grew various grains. The nearest school at the time was in Bayamo, and the only available means of transportation was on horseback. I began working on the farm as a young boy, and for this reason my formal education ended with the fourth grade of grammar school. I met Estrella Vazquez Ramirez in Manzanillo, a seaport in southeastern Cuba, and we were married in that city. Later we returned to the family farm near Cauto. A man who repaired the artesian well on our farm frequently spoke of economic opportunities available in the United States. My father, who had visited the United States, also encouraged me to migrate and repeatedly told me, "That's the land of opportunity—go over there and seek your fortune. If it doesn't work out, then you come back."

Heeding their advice, I arrived in the United States in September 1943. My wife had attended school in New Orleans and had relatives living in the city, so I decided to settle there. She did not accompany me on the trip but remained in Cuba with our daughter, Estrellita, who was a year old. Subsequently Estrella came to New Orleans, and our other two children, Tania and Robert, were born in this country.

My first job was with Segundo Brenes Navarro, a Puerto Rican who owned International Express Company, a freight-forwarding business located in downtown New Orleans. Initially Navarro paid me $12 a week. I worked for him for five months, until the company relocated to New York. Although Navarro asked that I join him in New York, I remained here because I did not want to move to a colder climate. The headquarters of the Latin American Chamber of Commerce was located at the same address as Navarro's firm, and I became friendly with personnel in the organization, including the president, a Colombian named Hernando Ramirez. They helped me by providing free lodging and directed me to Graham Paper Company, where I found a job as a laborer in their warehouse, earning $120 a month.

In the beginning I did not speak English and none of the employees spoke Spanish, so I made my wishes known through sign language. For the same reason it was difficult to order food in a restaurant. I would go to a counter, rather than a table, and the waitress would say, "What do you want?" I would see what the people next to me were eating and point to their food, because I did not know how to say, "The same thing." I ate what other people liked, but it kept me going. Later I became close friends with Hernando Ramirez and his wife, Dora, who was from Puerto Rico. We dined often, and they taught me how to order food in English.

New Orleans in 1943 was quite different from the way it is today. For example, the Spanish community was small. You sounded like a stranger if you spoke Spanish on a streetcar or in a restaurant, and everyone would look at you. The port of New Orleans was very active, especially during the time the port of New York was not accessible to commercial traffic.[1] When the port [of New York] reopened, the Latin American Chamber of Commerce and many freight-forwarders working in New Orleans moved to New York.

In 1955 I decided to leave my job at Graham, where I had worked for 11 years, and became a sales representative for some paper mills. My wife engaged a young Cuban woman to care for the children, and with limited savings we started our company. For two years I exported paper to Latin American companies and imported art supplies. At the time, I was a member of the Export Managers Club of New Orleans and was friendly with members of the consular corps. At one of their gatherings Ted Di Marzio, who was serving as Italian trade commissioner, mentioned that the owner of Industrie Lazzaria Spa-Spresiano was looking for a local distributor for his picture-frame moldings. He suggested that it might be profitable for me to import picture frames while I exported paper. I met the company representative, who was a charming person, and agreed to represent the organization. As this new area of business became lucrative, I gradually withdrew from working with paper mills and art supply companies, and by 1957 our operation focused entirely on picture-frame-molding distribution. In time we began production of custom-made frames. Most high-quality moldings that require intricate handwork come from Italy, Austria, Germany, and the Orient, so I travel to those places every year. Now I include Guatemala in my flight schedule, as we are distributors for moldings made from Guatemalan wood and manufactured by Maymo. However, we also make frames from ash, which is an excellent American wood.

In 1986 we moved to our present facility, which is located on land owned by the New Orleans Dock Board. I lease the land but own the buildings. I chose this large facility so that we could easily expand our holdings. Although I could have moved to the suburbs, I enjoy working in the city and particularly in this area that is close to the Mississippi River.

Over the years, I witnessed sizable growth both in the city's economy and in the Hispanic community. Now I would like to see greater expansion at the port of New Orleans. At one time New Orleans was the second largest port in the country, but over the years we lost business due to lack of initiative by top management. During the same period port management and freight-forwarders in Miami were campaigning aggressively for firms in Venezuela, Guatemala, and Costa Rica to send their cargo through the port of Miami. I don't feel it is sufficient for the mayor of the city and his entourage to visit a Latin American country and come back with promises. We need a permanent government agency to promote trade with Latin America. Our port has much to offer. Geographically, it only takes two days to ship cargo from New Orleans to Central America, while it takes six days to travel by boat from Miami to Central America. We have dock facilities, rail lines, trucking companies, and a good port manager, Ron Brinson. We need someone in local government to create the business and organize it.

I have been thinking about retiring for some time, but it is difficult. Instead, I intend to slow down. I have a fine son who manages the business and is capable of creating unlimited future growth. Yet there are areas where I can still help the organization, and I will remain here but take more time off to relax. I like gardening and look forward to traveling around America, for there is much to see in this country.

What I enjoy most in business is the challenge of solving daily problems. I get credit for being very successful, and I am very happy with my accomplishments. But I believe the reason a person is successful is due in part to the amount of determination he has in applying himself. You have to want to reach a certain position in life. You choose a business and then work hard—mornings, afternoons, and nights; Saturdays and Sundays. If you follow these suggestions, I feel that you will attain your goal.[2]

SUSANA PEÑALOSA HURTARTE

I think our [Hispanic] community is coming of age. There are more professional groups and organizations that are active now than ever before. Lately the organizations have focused on economic development and political growth, rather than social recreations or soccer games. Not that I am against entertainment or anything like that, but I think it shows maturity. Every day we are getting more involved, more courageous in voicing our opinions, and now we have a weekly column by Octavio Nuiry [the featured columnist of "Nuestro Pueblo," reporting on activities in the Hispanic community] in the Times-Picayune. *I think that says a lot for us.*

Susana Hurtarte believes that in the near future Hispanics will serve as elected officials in the Greater New Orleans area. Since her arrival in Louisiana in 1969, she has identified closely with the Hispanic community and contributed to its economic prosperity. She initiated business seminars conducted in Spanish and trade fairs exhibiting services and products available from Hispanic-owned businesses. Hurtarte inaugurated annual recognition of Hispanics living in New Orleans who made distinguished achievements in education, economic development, health, civic improvement, the arts, and culture.[1] She welcomes similar presentations currently bestowed by other organizations, remarking, "I don't think it really matters what the awards are called, as long as outstanding Hispanics are being recognized."

At my initial meeting with Hurtarte in 1986, she and an associate managed the Americas Group, a public relations and marketing organization that was funded by the U.S. Small Business Administration and guided Hispanics starting or expanding businesses. At the time, she was a single parent with two sons. By our next meeting, held in 1989, she had remarried and was working with her husband in creating sophisticated new markets for products imported by their company from Latin America.

Hurtarte's delightful sense of humor has helped her adapt to many professional and personal changes, and she remains a poised woman with sharp business instincts.

My parents were very involved in civic affairs in Tijuana, Mexico. For many years, my father was a volunteer and officer with the local Red Cross chapter. My mother was active in bringing about needed social reforms. During the 1950s, while visiting a maid's relative who was in prison, she became aware that unwed mothers were incarcerated with their children. The children were dirty, suffered from malnutrition, and some were ill. Further investigation revealed that, once released from jail, [these mothers] would invariably commit other crimes to support their family and would return to prison. My mother started a vigorous campaign to alert state officials to the need for retraining these women so that they could lead productive lives. A government program was enacted that included teaching them basic reading, writing, hygiene, health, and child care. For those capable of higher education, courses were available in typing, shorthand, and bookkeeping. She was also responsible for the creation of free breakfasts for indigent children. Her work evoked much criticism in the community, but it eventually led to the adoption by state government of other needed social services.[2]

Being born in Tijuana can be an unusual experience. The city was founded by a woman who became wealthy selling liquor to American servicemen stationed in San Diego, California. During Prohibition men would cross the Mexican border and buy alcohol at local bars. As the town grew, two distinct and separate societies emerged: one that was non-drug-related, and [one that] survived entirely on drug-related activities. Although I was brought up as *una niña appropriada* [a proper child], I saw persons in the city who existed totally under the influence of drugs, and consequently I could never be enticed to use them. My father owned a small advertising and public relations firm. Previously he worked both as a radio announcer and head cashier at the Caliente Race Track. I attended primary and secondary schools in Tijuana and studied business administration at San Diego State College in California.

While attending college, I met my first husband, a Louisianian who was stationed with the U.S. Navy in San Diego. We married in 1969 and moved to New Orleans after his discharge from the service. Upon my arrival in the city, I was hired by Avondale Industries as an interpreter for the many Cubans employed at the shipyard as plumbers, pipefitters, and welders. Officials at Avondale considered them reliable workers and wanted me to assist them in overcoming language as well as cultural problems. Some Cubans had experienced repression under Communist rule for many years prior to their arrival in the United States. They thought that they were now living in a free country where they could do anything, from having three wives [to] claiming them on their W-2 forms.

I left Avondale when I became pregnant and thought that I would devote my life to being a good wife and mother. On several occasions clients and business associates of my former employer asked me to substitute for their Spanish-speaking personnel who were either ill or on vacation. I soon recognized the need for an employment agency, similar to Kelly Services, that would provide substitutional bilingual personnel to industry, and opened Multi-Lingual Temporary Service with a partner in 1980. Our office was located at International House in New Orleans, and our staff included persons who could produce translations in several languages and clerical workers assigned exclusively to oil-related companies. The firm was profitable until

1984, when many clients withdrew from our services due to losses sustained from decreased oil prices. By coincidence, at the same time my partner and I went through successive divorces and decided to close the company for financial and personal reasons.

During the time I was at International House, I joined the Latin American Chamber of Commerce. At one of their meetings the district director of the U.S. Small Business Administration asked the audience for suggestions to increase Hispanic participation in their programs. I began relating negative experiences shared by Hispanics in the past. At his request I sent him a report outlining ways to improve relations with Hispanic entrepreneurs through uncomplicated methods of counseling. The report was forwarded to their headquarters in Washington, D.C. SBA provided a grant to implement the program through the establishment of the Americas Group. An associate and I were assigned to head the agency, whose main task was to provide, at a nominal fee, listings of resources and literature applicable to the individual needs of Hispanics wishing to start or expand an existing business. The information was drawn from local, state, federal, and private organizations. In 1986 we sponsored a business development seminar and trade fair that later became an annual event known as Latino. The first conference consisted of workshops on marketing, banking, international trade, career improvement, and a trade fair. Over 250 persons attended the meeting. Because the event has grown in scope and attendance, the third annual conference, held in 1988, included the Louisiana Hispanic Chamber of Commerce as one of its sponsors.

In 1987 I married Mario Hurtarte, a civil engineer who was born in Guatemala. He started an export-import company, National Enterprises, in 1981, that supplies agricultural and industrial machinery to firms in Central and South America. The company serves as subcontractor to the Agency for International Development. National Enterprises was one of my first clients at Multi-Lingua. We began a good professional relationship that flourished into friendship and ended in marriage. Dealing in international trade, I find there are two major problems that we must constantly address. Because of limited demand for cargo ships, there is no direct service from Central and South America to New Orleans. Currently one or two ships with refrigerated containers arrive weekly from Central and South America; however, they stop in Miami before arriving in New Orleans. When the cargo arrives in the city, it is over 10 days old and it becomes a precarious situation if you are dealing with fruits and vegetables. Another problem we face is in financial transactions. Most of us have to work with banks in Monroe, Louisiana; Houston, Texas; or Miami, Florida because there is not a true international bank here in New Orleans. No matter how often persons in the industry complain, we have not been able to effect any changes. Perhaps we need a representative group of true entrepreneurs from the private sector to voice our needs to the government, rather than through politicians.

My husband and I feel that growers in Central America traditionally receive little compensation for their crops. For the past two years my job at National Enterprises has been to develop new, sophisticated marketing for nontraditional items, such as more perishable fruits and vegetables not handled by multinational shipping firms. If we are successful with our marketing, we feel that not only will growers receive higher prices for their products, but a better trade relationship will develop between Central America and the United States. I have found a handful of American investors and businessmen who share this dream, and we will work with them to make this dream possible. I have had many pleasant experiences living in New Orleans, but I was happiest when I was recognized not as a leader but for my work and contributions to the community as a whole.[3]

ERNESTO SCHWEIKERT III

Anyone who is willing to work at developing an opportunity will find them available in New Orleans.

Ernesto Schweikert came upon an untapped source of income when he noticed that many Latin American tourists in New Orleans required assistance in arranging for transportation or tours or in making dining reservations. At the time, he was employed at a large travel agency and related the information to his supervisors. Since the company failed to develop this market, Schweikert opened a small travel office in his home. The agency began in 1976 under the name Iberoamericana Tours, and its services were intended to provide Hispanic tourists with a carefree visit to the city. In the beginning Schweikert focused on meeting tourists at the airport and providing them with transportation. Then, over 15 years, he added new services, changed the company name to ABA Tours and Travel, and increased his office space. Currently there are two offices in New Orleans; one in Houston, Texas; and another in Guatemala City, Guatemala. He looks forward to expanding his business nationwide.

Similarly, when Schweikert learned that KGLA—the only Spanish-speaking broadcasting station in the city—would be sold, he formed Crocodile Broadcasting Corporation (CBC) and purchased the station. As president of CBC, he plans to increase the listening audience to include Latin American countries.

Ernesto Schweikert's demeanor belies his adventuresome spirit. He is a soft-spoken young man with an unassuming manner. He came to the United States from Central America as a teenager and attended school in New Orleans. When he finished his studies, he accepted an offer for employment in his homeland. There, however, he found the political climate unsettling and returned to New Orleans, where he felt certain he would succeed in his profession. He considers the city charming and is well versed in its history, culture, and commerce. He sees the locale as an ideal vacation area for Latin Americans and would like to increase tourism from every Latin American country so that New Orleans may once again become "The Gateway to the Americas."

Although my parents, sister, and I were born in Guatemala, our ancestors came to Central America from Italy, Spain, Germany, and New Orleans, Louisiana. My sister, Maria Elena, and I were educated both in Guatemala and the United States. When we were teenagers, we came to New Orleans and stayed with a family friend who took care of us while we completed our education. I worked part-time at a travel agency and drove the courtesy car that picked up tourists at the airport. Occasionally I would arrange sight-seeing tours for Hispanics visiting the city. I became aware that these tourists also needed help in making hotel and dining reservations, confirming their return flight, and arranging to have baggage shipped home. I suggested to my supervisor that the agency would increase their business if they opened a Latin American department and offered these services, but company officials were not in favor of the expansion.

At the time, I did not have sufficient experience in tourism, but I decided to open a small travel agency in my home. I started in partnership with my former wife and another associate.[1] We named the firm Iberoamericana Tours to appeal to travelers in New Orleans from Spain, Portugal, and Latin American countries. The company succeeded because I chose the proper strategy and my associates were helpful and competent. We moved our headquarters to an attractive but modest space in the French Quarter. Later we rented office space on Canal Street, where we extended our services from receptive tourism, which is basically greeting travelers at the airport, to include retail and wholesale tourism. When we sell a single airfare ticket, we refer to the sale as retail tourism. We carry on wholesale tourism when we put together package trips that include the cost of air travel, hotels, and tours. Before we specify a competitive price for a trip, we negotiate the cost for each item with companies that provide these services and add a commission fee for the agency that sells them. We specialize in package trips to Mexico, Guatemala, and Costa Rica.

To remain competitive in the field of tourism, I spend half of my life traveling to new places and meeting new people so I can fashion package trips that will motivate travel. When I put together a trip, I work many hours and employ creativity to produce a valid product. I apply the same meticulous care to details whether the tour is directed to an individual or to a group of conventioneers. There are now 11 companies in New Orleans that provide services similar to those we perform. Therefore, in order to appear as the first entry among travel agencies alphabetically listed in the telephone directory, I changed the company name to ABA Tours and Travel. The letters *ABA* stand for "American Best Airlines," and it is an easy name to pronounce, both in English and in Spanish. Those currently interested in started a travel agency should not only have experience and ample financial backing but need to bring a new service on the market. In this manner they will eliminate competition from an established agency that has developed good commercial ties and whose credibility has been substantiated over the years.

In reality, my business consists of delivering service, because we do not own airline companies or hotels. For this reason we treat our customers with courtesy and furnish our cars when we take them to or from the airport. Additionally, if clients prefer to transact their business in a language other than English, our office staff is prepared to converse with them in Spanish, French, Italian, and German. Presently we have offices in New Orleans,

Houston, and Guatemala City. In the future I would like to establish a network of travel agencies throughout the United States in cities with sizable Hispanic populations. Each office would be treated as a franchise corporation. It would be an ideal investment for young couples who enjoy travel and public relations, and if the agency is well managed it will provide good financial returns.

My initial contact with radio station KGLA came about when I used their facility to advertise our travel services. I worked closely with Julio Guichard and Alberto Carillo, who were the only Hispanics in the partnership company that owned the station. I collaborated with Julio Guichard on many projects and every year provide travel arrangements to entertainers who appear at El Festival de la Canción, a festival sponsored by the radio station. When Guichard notified me that KGLA would be offered for sale, I contacted local business associates and family members in Guatemala and raised the required capital. We named the new partnership the Crocodile Broadcasting Corporation (CBC) because this reptile is native to Louisiana and Latin America and shared in both cultures. A caricature of the crocodile will be featured in our advertising campaign.

As president of CBC, I frequently meet with Julio Guichard and Alberto Carillo—who are also partners in the new company—to talk over proposed undertakings for KGLA. We plan to gradually increase our programming until we have extended to continuous, 24-hour broadcasting. Currently radio signals are weak in sections of the city; therefore, we need to increase our power capability from 1,000 watts to 10,000 watts—the increased wattage will permit the broadcasts to be heard clearly throughout the area. Next, we foresee presenting simultaneous programming from New Orleans to Mexico, the Caribbean region, Central America, Venezuela, and Colombia by means of shortwave transmissions. The programs would serve as an avenue for advertising Louisiana—its products and tourism. For example, the added publicity, along with current available daily air travel from Mexico to New Orleans and the state's tax exemption program for foreign tourists, would bring additional Mexican travelers to the city.

Concurrently we will attempt to increase the size of our local audience. We will start a series of programs that will appeal to Anglo listeners. The radio announcers will be bilingual and will play music performed by well-known celebrities, including Julio Iglesias and Gloria Estafan. We have commissioned a study to learn the habits and life-styles of different classes within the Hispanic community. After we have analyzed the data, we will prepare a schedule compatible with the needs of the community. The membership of a proposed KGLA listeners club will receive monthly bulletins listing our schedule.

Over the years, my friend Romi Gonzalez and I have shared similar ideas for developing tourism from Latin American countries to New Orleans, and we believe that music serves as a common bond that joins Latinos. We originated the idea of presenting a music-and-heritage festival in the city. Now in its third year Carnaval Latino is growing in popularity and we firmly believe it will become a tradition in New Orleans.

I have other projects in mind that I would like to accomplish during my lifetime. Although the future seems very distant, perhaps in 10 years some of these undertakings will have been achieved. I intend to finance them through my work—but labor has never bothered me, because it is recompensed with money.[2]

JOSÉ (PEPE) VASQUEZ

When I arrived in New Orleans, I spoke only Spanish. I learned welding and supported my family by working in a job where knowledge of English was not essential. However, I always hoped that someday I would own my business and become a somebody in this country.

In 1977 Pepe Vasquez opened Vasquez Supermarket, financed by a loan from the U.S. Small Business Administration. He then opened a restaurant and later an auto-parts store. And although he organized the musical group Ritmo Caribeño for personal enjoyment, it too became a business venture.

Vasquez is part of a large extended family that left Cuba in small groups during the 1960s and settled in New Orleans. Family members share in his enterprises: his wife and younger son work in the supermarket; his older son and a daughter manage the restaurant; a brother runs the auto-parts store; and another brother and son perform with the musical ensemble. Vasquez is proud of his Cuban heritage. Formerly he was president of Liceo Cubano José Marti, a social club organized to preserve Cuban culture in New Orleans; currently he is president of both the José Marti Monument Foundation, established to erect a memorial in New Orleans in honor of the Cuban patriot and author, and the Spanish American Business Association, a professional club that fosters unity among Hispanic entrepreneurs.

Pepe Vasquez was cordial during our two meetings held in his supermarket but remained aware of what was occurring in the store and would often pause during our conversation to resolve apparent problems. As a rule, he works between 14 and 16 hours a day. When asked how he maintained this strenuous work load, he replied, "I have always been an active person. I detest being lazy."

My parents were born and lived in Mariel, a city located in the province of Pinar del Rio in Cuba. They raised a family of five sons and three daughters. My formal education ended when I was 14 years old and went to work on the family farm. I also worked in the asphalt mines. Mining was an important industry in Mariel at one time, but when the asphalt recovered decreased in quality, mining operations were moved to other locations and the mines were closed. However, agriculture, and in particular the sugar crop, remains the major source of income for the area. Another job in Cuba included working as a maintenance mechanic at Terma Electrica, a public utility plant.

I never intended to leave my country. But living conditions swiftly became intolerable under the communistic government of Fidel Castro, and I decided to immigrate to the United States. I joined other family members who had previously fled Cuba and settled in New Orleans. In 1969 I arrived in the city with my wife, Adelina, and two children, José and Ada. (My younger son, David, was born in New Orleans.) I found the city to be exactly as described in correspondence from friends and relatives and consequently adapted quickly to the new surroundings. Although I did not speak English, I found a job where I learned welding and from 1969 to 1977 supported my family with this skill.

However, I wanted to be self-employed. With a $50,000 loan acquired from the U.S. Small Business Administration, along with assistance from my brother, Pelayo, and my father, Tomas, I opened a neighborhood supermarket. It was a new undertaking, but I knew that if I added a predetermined sum for operational costs to the price of each item, the business would succeed. I stock a variety of canned and frozen products, foods indigenous to Latin America, meats, poultry, fish, produce, and sundry items. Over the past 14 years I've developed a steady trade with Hispanics and Anglos who shop at the supermarket.

My other commercial pursuits started in response to needs expressed by family members. In 1985 my older son, José, graduated from high school. He did not choose to continue his education but wanted to manage a business. He asked for direction, and I suggested that a restaurant would be a lucrative undertaking, since everyone has to eat. I found an excellent rental site and signed a long-term lease. José was 17 years old when we opened Vasquez Seafood Restaurant, but he handled responsibility commendably and worked long hours to make it a profitable investment. He employs a staff of eight workers, including my daughter, Ada. As a rule, most patrons come during the lunch hour. The menu lists a variety of hot meals; however, seafood remains [one of] the more popular items requested, whether it is served in a sandwich or as part of a combination platter. And home delivery has become a popular service, used by many regular customers.

In 1988 the store next to my supermarket became vacant. I rented the space to open Vasquez Auto Parts Store and utilize the services of a brother who was unemployed. Although Ricardo is familiar with the merchandise and is a competent manager, the store has not been as profitable as the other businesses. Major factors contributing to this dilemma include a lack of cash flow, prompted by an expensive inventory that is stored to meet customer needs, and the inability to compete with lower prices offered by dealers affiliated with national distributors.

Each business is handled as a separate corporation. I serve as president of the three companies but for the most part work in the supermarket. I am available for consultation and remain vigilant to changes that may occur in operating costs. I work closely with my bookkeeper, who understands our operation and recommends changes or adjustments whenever they are needed. I do not intend to open another business in the near future, because operating costs have risen excessively and competition has increased. I enjoy my work, but it is tedious dealing with the public. Whenever I come across an unpleasant situation with customers, I attempt to clarify the misunderstanding quickly and reestablish good relations before they leave my establishment.

In addition to my companies, I perform with the musical group Ritmo Caribeño and serve as their manager. When I was 15 years old, I played percussion instruments with a group called Jovenes de las Minas and enjoyed performing whenever we received engagements. My interest in music was rekindled in 1980 when a brother who is a musician came to New Orleans. We organized a four-piece band and played for personal gratification. But music is like honey and musicians are like bees, and gradually we added six musicians to the group. We made our initial professional engagement in 1986. Our repertory consists of dance music popular throughout Latin America, to attract our multinational community, and our popularity has grown by word-of-mouth. Recently we were nominated for the "Big Easy" awards presented annually by a local newspaper. We accept engagements for private functions as well as for large gatherings. Every year we play at the New Orleans Jazz and Heritage Festival and Carnaval Latino. Outdoor festivals provide a close bond between performers and the audience that is not found in other settings. For a period we played on weekends in a local nightclub, but when the establishment was sold the new owner preferred different entertainment. As a rule, nightclubs where Latin American music is performed are short-lived and consequently musicians wishing to work full-time in this field move to other cities where more job openings are available. Recently we recorded a demonstration record to send to nightclubs in other localities, to obtain additional work. Many bands from Latin American countries use this method to publicize their music, and it has proven lucrative for them.

I intend to continue working with Ritmo Caribeño in the future, using it as a source of personal enjoyment and added income. However, the majority of my time will be devoted to managing the three companies so I may provide my family with a steady flow of financial support.[1]

3

ARTS IN A CARNIVAL SETTING

LAGNIAPPE

Under French and Spanish rule, Mardi Gras was celebrated with private balls and informal street revelry. Modern-day Carnival festivities can be traced to the 1857 establishment of Comus as a Carnival organization and to the subsequent formation of similar groups.[1] After club officials select a theme to highlight the year's Carnival celebration, artists are employed to translate the idea into different mediums, such as sketches and models of parade floats, costumes, and programs and invitations. These are in turn used by float builders, tailors, and printers to produce the finished product.[2]

Mardi Gras and other open-air festivities held in New Orleans serve as a stimulant to creativity among artists.

GEORGE FEBRES

The first member of my family came to Ecuador from Venezuela with Simón Bolivar's armies to take part in the war of independence from Spain. He was Lieutenant Leon de Febres-Cordero but, in typical Latin American fashion, became a general when he landed in Ecuador. He liberated Guayaquil, the largest city in Ecuador. Since then, the family produced many politicians, statesmen, cabinet ministers, writers and poets, a great many priests and nuns, a bishop, and even a saint. But we never had a president or an artist. Then in 1984, Cousin Leon [Febres-Cordero] became president of Ecuador. And now there is me.

Certainly George Febres, christened Jorge Xavier Febres-Cordero Icaza, comes from an illustrious family, but his own life reads like an immigrant success story. His occupations have included factory worker, busboy, waiter, maître d', U.S. Army draftsman, student, and University of New Orleans and Tulane University faculty member. Today a widely known artist, Febres from 1981 through 1984 ran an art gallery named after his French granduncle, Jules Laforgue, the symbolist poet who created free verse.[1] And Febres is also credited with being the creator, organizer, and driving force behind an emerging movement in contemporary art called "visonary imagism."[2] The movement combines superb craftsmanship, keen wit, and penetrating intellect.

Influenced by surrealism and symbolism, Febres in 1974 began transposing commonplace language into visual puns. His signature piece, Alligator Shoes, consists of a pair of women's shoes made of whole baby alligators, including the reptiles' heads, which form the toes of the shoes. Highly acclaimed for its originality, the piece has often been pictured in national and foreign publications and on television and is now on view at the New Orleans Museum of Art. Other well-known Febres pieces include Palm, a 12-foot tree, and Deviled Egg, commissioned by the White House for one of its annual Easter egg hunts. The latter piece is cataloged as a permanent holding of the Smithsonian Institution.

During our interview Febres—whose appearance reflects his distinguished parentage—provided humorous, thought-provoking, and always-candid answers, each underscoring his distinctive personality. He said, for example, that he used television programs as a tool for enriching his vocabulary and occasionally for inspiration. When a game-show host once characterized a contestant's answer as "two sandwiches short of a picnic," Febres so delighted in the phrase that he immediately used it as the title of one of his self-portraits. Similarly, his museumlike residence, which comprises a spacious studio, office, gallery, and two stories of living quarters, is filled with exotic artifacts (among them the skins and bones of dead animals and an assortment of stuffed birds and chickens), a dozen or more portraits of his canonized cousin, and, of course, scores of his own creations.

My background? OK. My father was born in Ecuador in 1906 and reared as a wealthy young man unaccustomed to work. In 1940 he married my mother, who was a beautiful, energetic woman. Both were artistic and had considerable creative imagination. My mother made her own hats and dresses, and my father made constructions out of cardboard. My brother and I were born in Guayaquil during World War II and grew up watching, alternately, Nazi propaganda films and American movies. Papa had spent all the money he had inherited, and my and my brother's only birthright was our eminent surname. But, fortunately, we also inherited our parents' artistic talents. As a child I made small drawings and paintings, and my brother worked at calligraphy. But he enjoyed sports more than art.

Shortly after my mother died of cancer in 1962, a letter arrived in the Guayaquil post office addressed to the local genealogy society, asking about a certain Ricardo Paredes. It was from Majorie Dixon Smith of Jackson, Mississippi. Because the president of the society knew that my father was a grandnephew of Ricardo Paredes, he turned the letter over to him. Mrs. Smith was ancestor-hunting: Ricardo Paredes, her great-grandfather, had left Ecuador in the early nineteenth century, come to New Orleans, translated his name to Walls, and settled down, eventually to fight for the South in the Civil War. Well, to make a long story short, she and my father struck up a genealogy correspondence, the upshot of which was that she invited him to send my brother and me for a visit with her. My brother left immediately, and I followed somewhat later, on 4 September 1964. Mississippi was a shock. I could speak only a few words of English I had picked up while working in an airline office in Guayaquil, but I could understand a good deal more—at least, I could in Guayaquil. But Mississippi was a different story. My cousin Majorie had a job waiting for me—another shock—in an aluminum sheet-metal factory, where she already had my brother working. Well, the workers there could not understand anything I said, and I could not understand anything they said. So I starting learning English all over again, this time with a southern accent.

After some months, my brother in 1965 moved to New Orleans and shortly afterwards invited me to join him. His apartment was in the French Quarter, and I arrived here the Friday before Mardi Gras. In Guayaquil Carnival is celebrated, but only in a minor way and almost exclusively by the lower class. And anyway, I had led a pretty sheltered life. I was amazed at the crowds and shocked at the nudity. But once I rose above my puritanical background, I loved it. I remember thinking, in my innocence, that this is what Disneyland must be like.

A year or so later my brother, always restive, felt the call of new adventure and joined the U.S. Air Force. Shortly afterwards I got a draft notice. The Vietnam War was raging at the time. So at the age of 22 I had to make a major decision. I had thought of myself as only visiting the United States but had made several close friends in New Orleans and was toying with the idea of staying. But did I want to stay at the risk of Vietnam? Yes, I decided, I did, and I went into the army on 12 May 1966.

During basic training I was stationed at Fort Polk, Louisiana. It was a trying experience because my English was still so very limited. Not only was it hard to understand the drill sergeant's commands, but I really could not read English at all. Consequently, I got one of the lowest IQ scores on record. As a result, when I finished basic training I was sent to Fort Bliss in El Paso, Texas, where my tasks were similar to those of a maid. I cleaned barracks and maintained a garden. In my spare time I amused myself by doing some little painting with watercolors. When one day a company sergeant happened to see the paintings, he recommended me for company draftsman.

My life changed completely with the new assignment. The soldier who was serving at the time as company draftsman trained me before he left, and a civilian who worked at headquarters corrected my misspellings. I made company charts and posters, and placecards for the commanding general's dinner parties. And eventually I painted murals in the mess hall. From that point on, my army life was a ball. It was, incidentally, during my time in the army that I simplified my name to George Febres. My full Spanish name, you see, would not fit on an army dog tag.

After receiving an honorable discharge in 1968, I went to Europe for the summer. I returned to New Orleans in the fall and enrolled in the fine arts program at the University of New Orleans, and worked as a student assistant in the history department. One of the students I met there was Alex (Alejandro) Bendaña, who later went back to his native Nicaragua to become a revolutionary.[3] Later I worked as desk clerk at the Maison de Ville hotel in the French Quarter and after that became assistant director of the Orleans Gallery. In 1972 I graduated from UNO and went on a teaching fellowship to Louisiana State University. To augment my income while there, I worked as a bartender at Dirty Pierre's tavern, where I decorated the bar with my drawings so that customers had the option of buying beer or a drawing, or both. It worked, and in 1974 I graduated with a Master of Fine Arts degree.

What artists have influenced my work? I could name 50 or more who have influenced me. They range from Arcimboldo through Magritte, Dali, and De Chirico to the fabulous Mexican artist Pedro Friedeberg. Pedro's signature piece is a chair in the shape of a hand. It is not merely clever but brilliant— a hand holding a human being! It evokes meaning on multiple levels, from "the hand of God" to "a bird in the hand." And, of course, it is masterfully crafted. My own work has similar "cerebral levels," as Mark Lussier called them.[4] Those artists I named all devoted their entire lives to art, something I respect and admire. I am also devoting my life to art, but I regard myself as only a beginner. I was 29 years old when I graduated from college and 31 when I finished my M.F.A. So I have had only 16 years as a developing professional artist.

Shows I have curated? Yes. I particularly enjoyed the one called "My Cousin the Saint." Born in Ecuador in 1854, Brother Michael, as he is known there, later became a member of the Christian Brothers order. He devoted his life to educating poor children. His was a full and giving life, and he left something on this earth. When it became clear, towards 1977, that he was going to be beatified and set on the road to sainthood, I got an idea. I distributed photographs of him to a number of friends who were New Orleans artists, asking them to do pieces on him. The exhibit, held in 1982, had the works of 40 artists represented—reflections on what being a saint means to the late-twentieth-century United States mind.[5] I am now thinking about doing a show on "My Cousin the President" to see what American artists will say about a Reagan-era president of a small South American republic.

My gallery? From 1980 through 1984 I ran a little art gallery [Galerie Jules Laforgue] devoted to the work of young artists. And I tried to be a real art gallery director. A real director has to do a great deal more than sell art, although that is important. A real director has to be able to spot talent early and develop it. That is the key. That is how really good gallery directors, of which New Orleans has had virtually none, contribute to the growth and development of art. The job requires not only a thorough knowledge and understanding of art but also an "eye," and that cannot be taught. It is a talent. I think I had it. I certainly judged the art of any artists, or would-be artists, who asked me to look at their work by the same standards I set for my own work. Frequently I told people they had no talent; often I pointed out what was wrong with works and how to improve them; and sometimes I actually showed them how to do it. That made a lot of people hate me, but at the same time it created closer bonds between me and those artists who had real talent. They appreciated what I was doing. They knew I was not being cruel but was trying to help them. And almost all have gone on to great success.

Changes in the New Orleans Hispanic community? I am not really familiar with those. My professional and social contacts have always been almost entirely with Americans, either artists or academics. Once in a while I will go to a reception sponsored by the consulate general of Ecuador, but rarely. When I came to the United States, I decided that if I was going to become an American, I would become an American; if I was going to change cultures, I would change cultures. So I conscientiously learned English, spoke only English, save on rare occasions, and Americanized myself, or at least New Orleanianized myself. I now think of myself as 100 percent American, not Ecuadorian. Ecuador was another, and now remote, part of my life. I do not mean to say that I in any way deny it. I do not. I value it and cherish it and constantly draw on it. It is part of me. But I am not an Ecuadorian; I am a New Orleanian American.[6]

MARGARITA BERGEN

I find that in [New Orleans] and in Louisiana there has always been a tradition of male chauvinism. It was difficult when I first opened this store. People would say, "Where is your husband? Who is the boss?" They thought there was someone else. But before long, people I knew [and] respected would come to me before they would do something and say, "What do you think of this?" Then I knew that I had made my place, and I am good in what I do.

†

Bergen Gallery deals in the graphic-arts work of well-known local and international artists. Its holdings include posters commemorating local events, such as the annual jazz festival, and illustrations associated with the decorative style of art deco. The gallery, whose market is geared to tourists and office interior decorators, is located in the French Quarter.

Gallery owner Margarita Bergen, a native of the Dominican Republic, arrived in the United States as a teenager. She attended high school in a predominantly Puerto Rican community in New York City and claims that she learned to speak English with a Puerto Rican accent. After her schooling she held responsible positions as teacher and administrator with the New York City and New York State departments of education. When Bergen first visited New Orleans, as a convention delegate, she enjoyed the city's cosmopolitan environment; hence she was delighted when, in 1979, she returned as an art dealer.

A gregarious woman, extremely proud of her heritage, Bergen was a delight to interview and provided candid answers. She considers it her responsibility as a citizen to become involved in local politics and has worked closely with elected officials in New York and New Orleans; on occasion she has been asked to run for public office. She is highly visible in the community, her name frequently appearing in print, both in the captions to photographs taken at charity fund-raisers and in feature stories discussing topics ranging from her childhood in the Dominican Republic to her 1961 Silver Cloud Rolls-Royce. During our interview she described herself as "two distinct persons—one who works extremely hard to sustain her business and the other who works just as hard enjoying life."

I remember an incident that took place while [I was] attending a reception at the presidential palace in Santo Domingo. I was chatting with a gentleman who said that my father was well known for his generosity. At one time, he recalled, Lorenzo Bergen supported 40 persons. My mother often spoke of my father's kindness, but I did not realize its far-reaching significance until I heard the story from a high government official.

My mother, Consuelo Suarez, was born in Santo Domingo and married my father when he was 60 years old. He was Cuban, and his brother, General Vincente Bergen, was involved with Máximo Gómez in revolutionary activities to gain Cuban independence from Spain. I was born in Santo Domingo and raised in La Romana, a community located in southeastern Dominican Republic. My father was a founding member of the community, and everyone treated us with great respect. Consequently, I grew up with the amenities of a wealthy child even though my father's fortune had been depleted. During a three-year span my mother lost her husband and Ramón Alfonso and Rafael Alfonso Suarez, her two sons from a previous marriage. My half-brothers died in an unsuccessful revolt against the government of General Rafael Trujillo. Owing to these tragedies, in 1957 my mother came to the United States to begin a new life. She arrived in New York with a temporary visa and worked for five years to save money for my passage and to establish permanent residency.

Prior to my arrival in 1962, I completed secondary education in the Dominican Republic, yet I was required to repeat some studies for local accreditation. I spoke very little English and attended public high school in the South Bronx, where there was a large Puerto Rican community. I joined Aspira, an educational organization formed to provide students of Spanish heritage with challenging intellectual experiences. As a member I was able to attend summer leadership training courses at Columbia University and met several political leaders.

After graduation I had a few routine clerical jobs. I had always been impressed with the swift pace of the stock market and was able to secure employment in the stocks and bonds department of several firms. I enjoyed the assignments but soon recognized that wherever I worked I was paid less than my male counterparts and was asked to train men who eventually became my supervisors. When I related the situation to one of my employers, he said that indeed I was a good worker, but felt that I would soon marry, because I was attractive, and retire shortly thereafter. Furthermore, he said, the young men I trained were Vietnam veterans and future breadwinners who would remain with the company for a long duration. I knew that I could find another job in the stock market, but I realized the only way I could compete as an equal in any field would be with a college degree.

I enrolled at City College of New York, initially attending night classes while working during the day. Later I enrolled in day classes and worked at night. Remembering the difficulty I encountered as a high school student with a limited English vocabulary, I chose bilingual education as my college major so I could help students with similar problems. Initially I received an associate degree in education, then a B.A. in secondary education, followed by an M.A. in bilingual education.[1] For several years I taught Puerto Rican students enrolled in junior high schools in the New York public school system. I enjoyed teaching but preferred the interaction with parents and the community. I returned to school and received a license to work as a community relations supervisor with the New York State Department of Education. As associate of the Bilingual Bureau, I provided technical assistance to individual schools and school districts. In this capacity and through my involvement in civic organizations, I met several city officials and media personnel. I was offered to host a television program on channel 41 in New York. I wanted to do the show, but my supervisors said it would pose a conflict of interest as a state employee. I began to feel that I was losing my autonomy, I was losing myself, I had to be reserved as an educator. I needed a job [where] I, Margarita Bergen, could show my personality.

In 1978, after terminating a long relationship with my fiancé, I called my younger brother, who was an artist living in New Orleans, and told him that I needed a change. He remembered that we'd visited an art gallery on a previous visit to the city and how much I'd enjoyed the relaxed atmosphere of the shop in the French Quarter. Lorenzo suggested that I move there and open an art gallery. We opened a tiny gallery and both worked seven days a week for $75 so the money would remain in the business. It was not easy work but I loved it, especially dealing with the public. Later we moved to larger quarters on Royal Street. At present the local economy is depressed, due to deep losses in oil-related industries. Thank God the economy elsewhere is better! Many of our customers were transferred out of state, so we cannot depend on local residents.

But if you want to remain successful, you have to follow market trends. As a result, I am concentrating on selling higher-priced items. You buy less, but when you sell an item in that bracket the profit margin is larger. Wealthy customers want to buy items that are produced in limited editions, since they usually have better resale value. Last week we sold an item for $1,800, and in a week's time the price rose to $3,700. It's my job to track down similar items and buy them from galleries that have them at lower prices. It involves a great deal of networking with other galleries around the country. Most of my buying is conducted on the telephone, but twice a year I go to market shows in New York and Los Angeles. My biggest problem is keeping my inventory low so there is continuous cash flow.

I enjoy living and working in the French Quarter because I can walk to so many places. Now wherever I go I am known, but I worked hard to attain that recognition.[2] I am involved in many civic and business organizations and recently was elected president of the Royal Street Association.[3] I have gone on trade missions with other businesspersons and city dignitaries to promote tourism in New Orleans. Yet at the same time I feel we need to attract new industry so that our talented young people will not continue to leave the city.

I work with various Hispanic groups but find the community disbursed through the city and disunited; we come together only when there is a disaster like in Mexico, and then we share. However, local Anglo politicians are becoming aware of our large numbers and have courted Hispanic votes in recent elections.

Most of my time is spent working hard in the gallery or promoting civic improvements. But at the same time I feel it is equally important to have a busy social life. Unfortunately, I have had an unsuccessful marriage. Still, I enjoy going to the theater, attending Carnival balls [and] benefit dinners, and riding in my chauffer-driven Rolls-Royce. It is my way of rewarding myself. I find that I would never be able to work such long hours unless I rewarded myself—or else what is life for? I look forward to continued success and hard work. If I change my career again, it would only be for a job as enjoyable as this one. Someday I would like to have enough money to retire; then I would take off and entertain my many friends but be busy in many organization, like a little fly—that's me.[4]

MARIO VILLA

Photo by Josephine Sacabo

I want people to know that they should not settle for less than the best furniture on the market. What I try to do with my work is to make people's dreams come true. [For example,] people come here and tell me, "I have a dream that I was sleeping underneath a coconut tree. Can you do anything about it?" I say, "Yes, I can make you a coconut-tree bed—but without the coconuts, so they won't fall into the bed." So it's fun.

To the delight of the customer, Mario Villa carried out the fantasy by designing the coconut-tree bed. He enjoys working with assignments that seem impossible, for they become a challenge—"I like to try something different in life," he notes. Our meeting, while most productive, was held under chaotic conditions, with continual telephone calls and visits by customers. Yet Villa remained full of energy, enthusiastic, and unperturbed, as if to indicate that this situation was typical at the gallery. He carefully answered telephone inquiries, greeted incoming customers as if he'd been waiting for their arrival, and eagerly responded to my every question.

Villa was born in Nicaragua. He is slight, has an engaging smile, and still possesses the appearance of a young student. He enjoys being with people and feels "life is so wonderful if you take it as it is." His careers as gallery owner and furniture designer underscores this philosophy, since both aspects developed from chance happenings. His furniture is elegant and unique, combining elements of Greek, Roman, and twentieth-century art; most pieces give an illusion of antiquity because of their patina. Villa's work was featured at an exhibition in the Gallery for Applied Art in New York. His furniture has been purchased by businesses and individuals all over the world, and his success has enabled him, along with a partner, to open a second gallery in Chicago.

My grandmother's kin, the Arguello family, lived in Nicaragua for over a century, but my parents were forced to leave the country during the 1970s because of political turmoil. They now live in Key Biscayne, Florida. My father, Julio Villa, met my mother while studying architecture in Mexico City. He is Nicaraguan, and she is Mexican. I was born in Managua, Nicaragua, as were my two sisters and a brother. I attended schools in Managua that were managed by Spanish Jesuit priests and at 17 was sent to study in Somerset, England. I did not care for the school but enjoyed traveling through Europe. In view of the fact that I was not applying myself in my studies, my father sent me to the University of Kansas to study architecture. It was a cultural shock for a man who had been studying in Europe to go to the midwestern United States, so I returned to Europe. In 1973 I came to New Orleans on a family trip and decided to remain. I enrolled at the University of New Orleans, where I fell in love with the anthropology department. As an undergraduate student I studied one summer with Ignacio Bernal at the Museo Nacional de Anthropologia and made a comparative report on anthropological excavations in Central Mexico and Nicaragua. One of the findings showed that ceramics made in Nicaragua during the preclassical period were very much in demand throughout Central America.

I received a degree in liberal arts in 1976 and continued my education at Tulane University, where I studied architecture. Since I had been an art collector for many years and knew many local artists, I decided to open an art gallery in my senior year and work on weekends. It was located in the French Quarter in a friend's house that had once been occupied by William Faulkner. I was given available commercial space on the first floor of the building. In exchange for free space, I promised to catalog the Helena Rubenstein art collection that he owned. On weekends I would bring crazy art that my friends had created, and antiques, and sit on the steps of the house chatting with all the tourists. People would ask me why I was there, and I used to tell them stories. Once I told them that my godfather was William Faulkner and he had an affair with a Latin American maid and I was their son. Some would come back to visit with me just so I would tell them stories.

After receiving my degree in architecture, I continued full-time with the gallery until I was certain what direction I would take with my life. I knew that I did not want a regimented job, because I enjoyed the freedom of being my own boss. It was amazing that I survived the first year in business, because everyone said, "You won't last longer than six months." I did quite well and was able to move to larger quarters, first to another address in the French Quarter and then to my present location in uptown New Orleans. However, in 1984 I lost a great deal of money and knew that I would not be able to remain in business.

The Contemporary Arts Center was also experiencing financial difficulties at the time and asked me to be a contributor to their forthcoming fund-raiser, "Art for Art's Sake." I have always drawn, so I took one of my drawings and made it three-dimensional, first in cardboard and then in metal. That inspired me to continue and design my first table. It consisted of a metal base with a sculpture of a male and female representing a family experiencing adversity. Their arms were extended upward, and their hands held a glass tabletop. When my work was displayed at the exhibit, it became an instant success and I received orders for five tables. Later I sold two chairs I designed, and in 1985 I received a commission for 135 chairs from a local restaurant. To date I have filled orders for furniture pieces from businesses and individuals in New York, Los Angeles, and San Francisco, as well as from Japan, Switzerland, Denmark, and France. I have 12 employees working in the office and studio, and I subcontract the iron work.

It takes about 20 working hours to create a chair. Every night I draw for 4 or 5 hours and usually choose one or two chairs to reproduce. I work with fitting a chair as a dressmaker works with a dress. I feel a chair must be perfectly comfortable for people to sit on, and I keep making changes until it is satisfactory. I enjoy working with brass, steel, and iron and like combining different mediums. I started out designing a table; then I designed chairs, lamps, fireplaces, and complicated pieces that contain architectural designs. My work is full of history and full of excitement. I don't come out with the ideas; the ideas come to me because I have lived them before.

Present facilities at the gallery are quite ample, with the space divided into two parts. One contains my studio and an office; the other is used as a gallery to showcase the work of unknown Louisiana artists. I review slides submitted by artists, and every month I choose a person—who may be young or old—whose work has not been exhibited. Latin American artists expect me to show their work because I am Hispanic, but I always refer them to other galleries in the city. For example, the one across the street is devoted exclusively to the work of Spanish artists.[1]

I have lived in cities around the world, but I feel New Orleans is my home. However, when I first arrived I had an unfortunate experience at a local bank where I kept an account. I was young and on that occasion had long hair and wore shorts. When the teller saw the amount requested, he exclaimed, "You don't look like you have that kind of money!" and insisted that I produce three different kinds of identification. I only had my driver's license with me, but I could not believe that a young man would be treated in that manner because he did not live up to a teller's expectations. My lawyer closed the account, and it has been the only time in my life that I experienced prejudice. I think it is important for Latin Americans to unite and show the Anglo community the number of Hispanic businesspersons and professionals that are part of the city. They also need to work more closely with politicians so that the Hispanic vote will be acknowledged.

There are problems in the United States, like everywhere else in the world, but here the American dream is to make the individual successful, so that the whole society feels successful in a way. This approach produces better citizens. I wish I could reach those Americans who may be experiencing confusion in their lives, and recent Latin American immigrants, to tell them that everyone here has a chance.

I believe, being a Latin who goes from one crisis to another, that I will continue this way. My whole goal in life is just to keep going, to keep growing, to keep learning. The moment you stop learning, you become old and die. Who knows—maybe someday I will be able to publish a book of poetry and produce a film.[2]

4

PROFESSIONALS IN THE GATEWAY TO THE AMERICAS

LAGNIAPPE

The expression "Gateway to the Americas" was widely used during the administration of Mayor DeLesseps S. Morrison, who served from 1946 to 1961. To fill the void created by a decrease in cargo following the end of World War II, Morrison initiated a program to attract Latin American trade to New Orleans.[1] The phrase was used to emphasize the city's geographic proximity to Latin America. Today "Gateway to the Americas" is employed to symbolize the city's reemergence as a leading port for Latin American trade.

The trade Morrison promoted with Latin America also encouraged Hispanics to immigrate to the United States and settle in New Orleans. Many of these newcomers who arrived during the 1940s were from middle-class families and possessed a knowledge of English. They came to New Orleans to study at local universities and elite private schools. In time, some became permanent residents and joined existing professional organizations.[2]

SOFFY BOTERO

When I hire a carpenter, I know I will pay him a fair price for his services. With the money he may purchase goods, perhaps buy a pair of contact lenses at my clinic. Similar transactions throughout the United States shape a strong foundation for a fluent economy. To improve their economic system, Latin American countries need to balance the currently uneven distribution of money.

Soffy Botero, made this point when discussing a significant problem in Latin American countries. She indicated that wages paid for menial labor corresponded to the exploitation of workers. But, she added, a promising sign in Latin American economies was the growing number of professionals and businesspersons entering the middle class. During our meeting Botero, having lived more than 25 years in each culture, gave her appraisal of life in the United States and in Spanish America. She provided lively comments on ways of alleviating social and economic problems and frequently referred to education as a cure-all.

Born in Cali, Colombia, Soffy Botero completed medical studies at the Universidad del Valle in that city, but she has practiced medicine and has undertaken professorial assignments primarily in the United States. In 1964 she was an intern at New York Polyclinic Hospital. She did her residency in both pathology and ophthalmology at Louisiana State University School of Medicine in New Orleans, where she was subsequently named assistant professor of pathology, teaching from 1968 through 1983. Her subspecialty was cytopathology, and she traveled throughout the country giving courses in this subject. Botero has also participated in many research programs, including one on preventing cervical cancer through the use of Pap smears, an endeavor sponsored by the National Institute of Health. She holds diplomas from three American medical boards, in anatomic pathology, clinical pathology, and ophthalmology.

She is married to Alfredo Botero, an ophthalmologist, and the couple have two daughters. Together the Boteros maintain the Botero Eye Clinic, which has two offices in the Greater New Orleans area.

During our interview Soffy Botero spoke of the desire for achievement as an admirable quality in American culture, noting that professionals in the United States lost no time keeping abreast of new scientific evidence. Still, she said, this time-consuming dedication tended to override such persons' interest in events occurring beyond the confines of their discipline. Summing up attitudes toward work in both cultures, Botero remarked, "Americans live to work, and Latin Americans work to live."

I was born in Cali, Colombia. My mother, Belja Sanchez, was a homemaker, and my father, Eduardo Duque, was a businessman who imported construction supplies. I am the oldest of six children and have four sisters and one brother. In keeping with the previous practice in Colombia of restricting educational opportunities for women, Mother's education ended after completing the fifth grade of grammar school. However, she was bent upon educating her family so they would be self-supporting. From childhood our lives were planned around learning, and we were spared from completing household chores. I took an interest in medicine and became a doctor. The second child studied architecture. She married an American and has two children. They live in Colombia, where she works as an architect. The third daughter lives in Charleston, West Virginia, and is a physical therapist. The fourth child, a son, studied economics. He lives in Cali, owns a business, and oversees family interests. The fifth child studied law and is a judge in Cali. (Incidentally, judges are not elected in Colombia but are selected by members of the Supreme Court.) The sixth child recently completed studies in medicine and will be coming to the United States. Mother is pleased that her children are professionals. Over the years, educational opportunities for women in Colombia have improved considerably. When I graduated from college in 1964, there were a fair number of women students enrolled in medical school. Currently many Colombian women attend college.

In 1964 my fiancé, Alfredo Botero, left Colombia to continue medical studies in the United States and encouraged me to emulate him. I passed the test administered to foreigners wishing to continue postgraduate medical education in the United States. I was 25 years old when I started at New York Polyclinic Hospital, and invariably patients and their families mistook me for a nurse. At the time, I suspect, the general public did not respond favorably to women in supervisory roles.

I married Alfredo in 1964, and we moved to St. Louis, Missouri, where he began his residency in ophthalmology and I started mine in pathology. We remained in that city for two years, developing lasting friendships with medical students and local residents. Meanwhile, Alfredo's uncle joined the staff of the ophthalmology department at Tulane University in New Orleans. He informed my husband of their excellent program and asked him to visit the university with the notion of continuing his studies at Tulane. Dr. Allen, chairman of the department, had taught medicine in Cali, Colombia, as part of an exchange program with Tulane University. His research was primarily in the field of external eye diseases, a subject of particular interest to Alfredo. Dr. Allen accepted my husband as a resident at Tulane, and I concluded my four-year residency program at Louisiana State University's School of Medicine in New Orleans.

Upon graduation Alfredo went to work with a local ophthalmologist, and I accepted a teaching post as assistant professor in the pathology department of LSU. From 1968 through 1983, I taught courses on pathology to students studying medicine, dentistry, medical technology, and physical therapy. I was also director of the pathology department at the Eye, Ear, Nose, and Throat Hospital from 1978 to 1983. My subspecialty was cytopathology, and I was codirector of the cytotechnology school based at Charity Hospital. Later, courses taught at the school became the basis for an accredited university degree program.

Three years ago I returned to medical school to study ophthalmology. It was burdensome studying and taking care of my family. I graduated in 1986 and joined the staff of Botero Eye Clinic. Alfredo opened the clinic six years ago, and we have offices in two locations around the city. Forty percent of our patients are Latin Americans; the others are Americans. I enjoy daily contact with patients, a function of private practice; in pathology human contact was limited to faculty members and students. Both areas of medicine are stimulating, and if possible I would like to practice ophthalmologic pathology and engage in research as well.

Last year I visited Cali to evaluate a clinic where two cousins practice ophthalmology. While assisting them in surgery, I realized they lacked surgical materials that doctors in the United States consider standard medical equipment. Numerous surgical instruments are made in Colombia and are modeled after those available in the United States. Yet surgeons are knowledgeable and perform admirably with limited resources. However, private hospitals, such as the Fundación Sante Fe in Bogotá, have modern equipment and technology comparable to provisions found in American hospitals. Medical schools in Colombia are commendable but offer limited residency programs, and frequently students must support themselves during this period of medical training.

In the 1960s many foreign doctors who were educated in the United States worked in state and federally supported institutions. As student enrollment in American medical schools increased, resulting in a large pool of available native-born doctors, tighter immigration restrictions were placed on the number of incoming medical students. The concept of educating foreign students in American medical schools as a means of updating health procedures in other countries is noteworthy. But many foreign doctors, including Alfredo and I, chose to remain in the United States after completing medical studies here.

Initially our plans were to remain in New Orleans until we saved $10,000; then we would return to Colombia. We occupied an apartment in a suburb located on the west bank of the Mississippi River. After we set aside the desired sum, we decided to remain in the United States and bought a house within a short distance of our former apartment. In 1973 we had our first daughter, and the three of us traveled daily to New Orleans. To avoid commuting, in 1978 we purchased a house in the uptown section of New

Orleans. I particularly enjoy the neighborhood because it reflects the urbane quality of New Orleans. It is hard to buy a house in Colombia, since loans are not readily available and few families can afford to purchase property outright. Consequently, Colombians who purchase a house usually expect to remain in the same dwelling for the remainder of their lives.

I feel New Orleans shares similarities with cities in Latin America, resulting from early Spanish jurisdiction over both areas. When we moved to the city, friends invited us to dine and savor the local cuisine. It was a Monday, and to my surprise we were served rice and beans, a dish frequently prepared in Cali. Moreover, family ties similar to those shared in Latin American culture are visible to a greater degree in New Orleans than in other American cities of similar size. I also observe that former New Orleanians frequently return to visit the city. Indeed, Hispanics are habitual visitors to their homelands. In fact, whenever our family plans to visit Colombia at Christmastime, we book passage six months prior to the holiday to ensure transportation.

Because I studied medicine, for the most part in the United States I am comfortable speaking in English when performing professional duties. On the other hand, I prefer speaking in Spanish when conducting my private life. I know several Americans but always find myself inviting Latin Americans whenever I plan a gathering at home. I speculate the attraction arises from sharing a common language and experiencing similar problems. One of the more difficult tasks we as first-generation immigrants face in the United States is to infuse our heritage and language in our children. I hope my daughters retain this heritage.

In the future I would like to continue my work in pathology. I miss teaching and may return to LSU as a part-time faculty member. Because I have been totally involved with my family and professional work, I need to set aside time for community service. Consequently, I look forward to joining the ranks of volunteers who, by contributing a little of their time and effort, help create an improved environment in New Orleans.[1]

DAVID KATTAN

The Immigration Law of 1965 changed procedures for admission to the United States. Since there were few lawyers who spoke Spanish in New Orleans during this period, Latin Americans would come to my coffee plant and ask for assistance with their legal problems. In time, I left the business world and assumed a full-time law practice.

✳

David Kattan has enjoyed two successful careers—one in business, the other in law—as a result of unexpected events. His latest office contains objects that manifest ties to both undertakings. A handsome round table, formerly used by professional coffee tasters, serves as the focal point of his waiting room. A lamp fashioned from a coffee mill provides illumination for the clientele seeking legal assistance. Memorabilia cover the walls—a photograph of Kattan taken when he was president of the Export Managers Club (1952–53), for instance, and a certificate listing him as a founding member of the Louisiana chapter of the American Immigration Lawyers Association in 1971. Later during our interview I learned that Kattan had served as general chairman of the Eighth Mississippi Valley World Trade Conference, held in 1953, and spoken at meetings sponsored by the Virginia World Trade Conference, the St. Louis World Trade Club, the National Foreign Trade Club, and the Memphis World Trade Club.

Kattan was born in Honduras and has lived in New Orleans for more than 60 years. He has a law degree from Loyola University, is fluent in Spanish and English, speaks Arabic, and understands French. He married his secretary 43 years ago. Thelma Fos Kattan remained as his employee and currently works in the law firm, along with their eldest daughter, who serves as office manager. The Kattans have three children and six grandchildren. Thelma Kattan joined us during part of the interview. An attractive woman, she spoke of her membership in several civic organizations, though she seemed happiest when referring to her family and their accomplishments. Throughout our lengthy interview I was impressed by David Kattan's air of youthful vitality and seeming ability to thrive on his busy life-style.

My parents were born and lived in Bethlehem, Palestine, when it was part of the Ottoman Empire. They married and moved to Honduras, Central America, where my mother's brother resided. Father owned a coffee plantation and an export-import business and frequently traveled to the United States on business trips. I was born in San Pedro Sula, Honduras, and had three brothers and three sisters. We grew up in La Pimienta, a small town located about 60 kilometers from the coast. The first school in the region opened when I was 10 years old. My brother and I attended for three months, until Father sent us to study abroad.

We traveled to the United States and attended Holy Cross School in New Orleans, Louisiana. At the time, there were about 65 other Hispanic children enrolled at the boarding school. Although faculty members warned us to speak in English at all times, we always conversed in Spanish whenever we were a distance from them. Our social activities were rather limited, but as a result we graduated from high school with an excellent education.

I attended Loyola University for undergraduate and graduate studies and received a law degree in 1939. I intended to pursue a career as a diplomat and enrolled at Georgetown University. When World War II started, it appeared unlikely that I could enter this field and I returned to New Orleans to practice law. I established my law firm, which was located about 12 blocks from the old courthouse building in the French Quarter. Unfortunately, an injury sustained while studying in the library for my bar examination resulted in extensive surgery on my knee. It became impossible for me to walk any distance supported by crutches while balancing books and file folders. Since gasoline rationing limited daily use of cars and taxis, I decided to put aside my law practice until fully recuperated from the surgery. I opened an export-import office where I could conduct business over the telephone.

Much trade was diverted to the port of New Orleans during the early part of World War II to avoid the threat of attack by German submarines stationed along the eastern coastline of the United States. Accordingly, my small business grew as I imported a variety of items, such as sarsaparilla root, rice, ginger, and coffee from my father's plantation. Gradually I developed a coffee-roasting business and became the first company in the city to handle coffee from seed to cup. Father would grow, process, and forward the coffee to New Orleans, and I would roast, package, and market it. We sold it under several trade names, including Lake Breeze Coffee and Creole Delight. We packaged a special blend of coffee and chicory for a well-known coffee company and provided coffee to Angola Prison, Charity Hospital, and local supermarkets. Moreover, we were the first local company to import large quantities of African coffee. Our offices were located in the uptown area of New Orleans, and we employed 18 salespersons. Incidentally, during the 1950s the coffee trading center in New Orleans was located near this office; now the location is called "Attorneys' Alley." Fortunately, firms such as Folger's Coffee Company opened roasting plants in other parts of the city and coffee remains a vital commercial venture.

During the latter part of the 1950s the cost of green coffee rose exorbitantly. When the price rose to $3.43 a pound, local banks would not provide financial support for large transactions. As most of the orders I handled were sizable, I found myself invariably searching for funds to keep my business solvent.

In the meantime, large numbers of Hispanics were migrating to New Orleans. Those needing legal assistance found few lawyers in the city who spoke Spanish. Many would come to my plant, and I began to help them on a part-time basis. When it became unmanageable to run a profitable business and support a growing family, I chose to change professions. I continued running my coffee plant during the day, while at night I attended several refresher courses at Loyola Law School.

When I opened my law practice, schools did not offer courses on immigration law, but I found the Immigration and Naturalization Service most cooperative in litigations. I charged a nominal fee of $15 for identity cards used by aliens to attest to their residency in the United States, and business was brisk. Gradually immigration policies became restrictive and reached a crucial point with passage of the Immigration Reform and Control Act of 1986. For instance, a section in the law placed strict sanctions on employers who hired illegal aliens, and the amnesty provision broke up some households. I know of cases where entire families applied for amnesty. Some met the criteria outlined in the program and received amnesty, while others who did not qualify were deported. Furthermore, passage of the Immigration Act of 1990 limited time allotted for pleading a case and required aliens to leave the country when confronted with voluntary departure. If aliens failed to depart at the designated time, they would not be allowed to return to the United States for a period of five years. Prior to this law lawyers could petition and receive extensions on their clients' departure from the country up to the day of the final deadline. In the past foreigners would apply for and receive temporary visas to visit with relatives in the United States. Currently it is hard to obtain these documents, and therefore some illegal aliens come to the United States to visit with parents or children whom they have not seen in many years.

According to the Constitution of the United States, resident aliens living in the United States are guaranteed about as many rights as native Americans, the exceptions being that they cannot work in an environment sensitive to national security, vote, or serve as candidates for the office of the president. Therefore, aliens are subject to deportation only after a judge has ruled in this matter and after their lawyers have depleted all possible appeals. The government cannot legally detain resident aliens until they are found deportable by an immigration judge and only after exhausting appeals.

I have served as legal counsel for several persons detained at the facility located in Oakdale, Louisiana. When aliens from around the country were initially transferred there, their legal counselors faced problems in locating local lawyers who spoke Spanish. Attorneys in New Orleans who accepted these cases soon discovered that it was a losing proposition, both in money and time. At the start, suits must be filed at courts located in Alexandria or Lake Charles, Louisiana, since Oakdale is not under the jurisdiction of courts in New Orleans. Then all transactions, including preliminary examinations, must be conducted at the site, which is about a three-hour drive from New Orleans. The architecture of the installation has also posed serious problems. It was constructed as an attractive building complex, but unfortunately administrative offices and the courts were placed within the confines of the prison. During the uprising of 1987 Cuban prisoners set fire to the area, and many records were destroyed. As a result, litigations had to be reinstituted for many existing lawsuits.

I have worked for many years on civic improvement programs. I was president of the Honduran Society for 9 years and served as president of the Louisiana chapter of Immigration Lawyers in the United States for 10 years. I will always remain concerned with the welfare of the community, but I feel I should relinquish my leadership to others at this time. However, I do not intend to retire from my law practice. I like to keep busy. Besides, if I stayed at home I would limit my surroundings. Here I have the added pleasure of looking at beautiful women who pass by my office. I like that![1]

NANCY MARINOVIC

Most Hispanics residing in the United States who are not American citizens remain so either through ignorance of naturalization procedures or out of loyalty to their native country. They need to be reassured that it is possible to love both countries. In fact, they are helping themselves and their families once they become acquainted with American civics and get involved in its political process.

Nancy Marinovic came to these conclusions when examining the reasons behind low voter participation among Hispanics in New Orleans. Her investigation, part of a study on the community, revealed that few Latin Americans were naturalized citizens and an even smaller number were registered voters.[1] To halt this apathy, Marinovic, together with other civic-minded persons, created the Hispanic League of Voters in 1985. They scheduled meetings with aliens, instructing them on the logistics of obtaining American citizenship and counseling them on the importance of political involvement in championing legislation directed to Hispanic needs.

Marinovic referred to the area's Hispanic community as "the greatest invisible human resource in the state," adding that more than a third of the group comprise professionals, craftspeople, businesspersons, and managers. She pointed out that there were obstacles in identifying these Hispanics, since some possessed surnames not indigenous to Latin American countries, while others operated businesses out of their homes. To educate the Anglo community on services and products available from Hispanic-owned companies, Marinovic joined the Louisiana Hispanic Chamber of Commerce in 1985. As a member she promoted the selection of New Orleans as the site of the U.S. Hispanic Chamber of Commerce's 1989 convention. She served as president of both local organizations and remains active in promoting their endeavors.[2]

In 1980 Marinovic opened an architectural/engineering/planning company, generally believed to be the first in the area owned and operated by a minority woman. At speaking engagements she encourages women to follow her example and seek training in professions normally dominated by men.[3] Marinovic is self-assured and perceptive, equally at home engaging in lighthearted conversation with friends or officiating at business seminars. Whenever she comes across a problem needing to be addressed, she works hard until it's resolved. She believes Hispanics can function commendably in the United States by judiciously combining in their life-style the best elements of both cultures.

My brother, sister, and I were born in La Paz, Bolivia, a country with a sizable population of Indians indigenous to the region, yet ruled by a handful of nationals of European heritage. As a child I would become angry with some of the laws and social customs imposed on Indians. Gradually I realized certain social conditions were difficult to reverse, and as an adult I learned to appreciate my country to a greater degree. My parents, Jeronimo Marinovic and Corina Ribera, were born in Bolivia. Father's family emigrated from Yugoslavia, and Mother's ancestors were Spaniards. Both came from large households, so we have a large extended family dwelling in Bolivia. Father was a veteran of the Chaco War and a revolution that took place in 1952. He worked for the government, holding several ministerial posts and serving in the diplomatic corps. Since the family accompanied him on foreign assignments, we attended school in Chile, Argentina, Italy, and Brazil, as well as in La Paz. My initial visit to New Orleans was during Father's appointment as consul general, but in 1964 the family came to the United States, seeking refuge from a repressive military rule. I returned to Bolivia to continue my education and studied architecture and urban planning at the University of San Andres. While in college I married and gave birth to a daughter. However, I knew I would leave Bolivia after graduation, in view of the country's limited economic opportunities.

Although I did not speak English, I chose to settle in New Orleans with my family and a nine-month-old daughter. At the time, the Latin American Apostolate had not consolidated its referral service to welfare offices, and social agencies were not easy to discern. It was strenuous finding work through newspaper ads and locating day-care centers for my child, but I knew that eventually I would learn English and make myself understood by associates. I worked at Schwegmann Giant Super Markets, Elmer Candy Corporation, and several department stores. In the beginning I sensed prejudice whenever I encountered difficulty operating machinery and could not express my dilemma. But in the long run I became a stronger person because I had to prove to others that I was intelligent and persistent.

When I felt confident conversing in English, I applied for work in architectural firms. I began as a draftsman and slowly advanced to responsible positions. To better understand constructional systems in the United States, I continued my education at night and received a degree in architecture-engineering technology from Delgado Community College. Because of my interest in politics, I also studied political science at the University of New Orleans. While working at the architectural firm of Hayden-Billes Associates, I had the opportunity to work on several urban planning ventures and became head of their planning department. One of the more rewarding projects I managed for the firm was an economic feasibility and recovery program for Bogalusa, Louisiana.[4] Prior to 1979 economic prosperity in the small city relied on employment of its work force at Crown-Zellerback Corporation, a wood-processing company. When corporate executives modernized the facility with the introduction of new machinery, many jobs were eliminated and economic chaos spread throughout the region. The mayor commissioned Hayden-Billes, along with two other firms, to proceed with an economic study of the area and devise a recovery plan. I worked in Bogalusa for six months before the plan was completed. Once [the plan was] accepted and implemented, the city's economic base expanded with a variety of small industries in addition to Crown-Zellerback. In this connection South Central Bell has a directory assistance office in the city and employs many residents.

I left Hayden-Billes to become self-employed and in 1980 opened Enplanar, a name fashioned from words describing our services, namely engineering, planning, and architecture. I started with a partner and three employees; now, as sole proprietor, I employ several architects, engineers, and planners and have further expanded into hydrographic surveying. Taking into account that all federal projects require participation by minority firms, I apply for every job as either prime consultant or subconsultant to larger firms. Compensation for minority participation averages from 10 to 15 percent of the total allocation assigned to a project. Consequently, we work continuously on different jobs. Up to the present time Enplanar has produced over 180 architectural, engineering, and planning projects, such as park renovations for New Orleans and neighboring cities and architectural/engineering projects for the U.S. Naval Air Station in Belle Chasse, Louisiana, as well as providing architectural/engineering services in Latin America. Enplanar's bilingual capabilities opened doors with the U.S. Agency for International Development in various Central American countries where school facilities and reconstruction work to buildings damaged by earthquakes are needed. We have initiated feasibility studies for local and federal agencies on land use, zoning, environment, and transportation. With studies involving construction of hospitals, libraries, or comparable facilities, we provide demographics on potential sites.

Initially I opened Enplanar knowing the federal government favored small minority businesses. Through interest in expanding my company, I acquired particulars on federal programs available to minorities who own businesses, as well as for those planning future ventures. I acquired the knowledge because I was inquisitive but wondered if others in the Hispanic community were aware of existing federal programs. Upon investigation I found limited printed material describing these programs and observed the need to bring more Hispanics into mainstream America. With a group of concerned New Orleanians, I started the Hispanic League of Voters in 1985, to educate those who were not aware of advantages associated with becoming American citizens.

At the same time, I felt little was known about the Hispanic population in Louisiana and wrote a report based on a study of that group, covering issues of importance to them. I provided copies to candidates running for political office to acquaint them with our ethnic group. In this report I referred to government figures projecting a population of 800 million Latin Americans by the year 2000 in Central and South America and concluded that a portion of the population would continue migrating to the United States. I stated they would settle in cities similar to New Orleans, where there is an established colony, but not as concentrated as in Miami or Los Angeles. I brought up the need for government agencies to increase publication of bilingual information on available services for the ever-growing number of Hispanics arriving to the city. Additionally, to sustain a large pool of volunteers serving as Spanish translators, a central municipal office should be installed as a clearinghouse between volunteers and hospitals, government offices, and retirement homes.

In my report I also touched on international trade, an area of interest to many Hispanics and our civic leaders interested in economic development. When referring to foreign business, I included the port as well as consular corps located in the city, since both share similar interests. In essence, a consulate serves as a notary office for a foreign country, recording documents on cargo entering or leaving a specific port. Once port traffic is reduced, as in the case of New Orleans, then the consulate's work load is also decreased. However, a new source of port traffic could develop if city officials extended greater hospitality to members of the consular corps. A consul general as a representative of a country is a guest in the city for two or three years, and if he or she does not feel welcomed, he or she will perform only required duties. Notwithstanding, I have known consuls who, through mutual agreement with regional consuls originating from the same country, shift portions of cargo to other host cities that offer greater incentives to their countries.

Although I was honored to serve as honorary consul general of Bolivia in New Orleans, I do not share in my father's keen interest in Bolivian politics. Rather, I want to develop trade between Louisiana and Bolivia and other Latin American countries and help small businesses identify available federal programs and economic development activities. For this reason I joined the Louisiana Hispanic Chamber of Commerce. Membership includes Americans as well as Latin Americans. The LHCC offers information on how to approach the Hispanic market, thereby serving as a bridge between Hispanic and American business communities. Its future goals include establishment of an international trade center in New Orleans to exhibit and sell products between Latin American countries and the United States.

After my arrival in New Orleans, I married David Sutherland, an American and native New Orleanian. My daughter, Carolina, is now 23 years old. Although she is an American citizen, she is bilingual, proud of her Bolivian ancestry, and favors Hispanic culture. She studied ballet for many years and attended Mercy Academy in New Orleans and a high school of performing arts in Natick, Massachusetts. Later she traveled to Russia and visited with the Bolshoi Ballet. She worked in New York for a while pursuing a career in ballet. At present she resides in New Orleans and is studying psychology at the University of New Orleans, and shortly will continue graduate studies in neuropsychology.

At speaking engagements I have been asked to comment on the role of women in the business world. Whenever I do, my mind reverts to what I have been able to accomplish in this country and [I] realize that it was due to opportunities offered to all in this great nation. If you are persistent and observant, utilize your knowledge and intuition, and work hard, you can make it in the United States. I thank this country, its Constitution and its laws, for allowing me to attain my aspirations.[5]

SALVADOR LONGORIA

I find decisions that are made concerning the Hispanic population in the country disappointing. One day I would like to become involved at the policymaking level in Washington and contribute my input to future legislation.

Salvador Longoria can be counted among a current group of young Hispanics in the United States who are successful professionals and participate in numerous civic undertakings. Recently the Louisiana State Bar Association named him "Outstanding Young Lawyer of 1991." Locally he serves in various charitable, political, and social organizations, including the Latin American Apostolate and the Jefferson Parish Public Schools Bilingual Education Program/Hispanic Parents Group. At our meeting he was friendly and forthright in his responses and spoke in detail about some of the prevailing organizations and committees formed to aid the Hispanic community.

Longoria was born in Cuba in 1958 and has lived in New Orleans since 1962. He was educated at parochial grammar and high schools throughout the city. During college he developed close ties with other Hispanic students, prompting him to reidentify with his Cuban heritage. At our session he described himself as a liberal Republican and said he had joined the Republican party when he was 18. Starting out as a volunteer at a local headquarters, he rose to the position of state chairperson and legal counsel for the Louisiana Republican Hispanic Assembly.[1] He enjoys politics and played an active role at the Republican National Convention held in New Orleans in 1988. Because of his many civic commitments, Longoria leads a limited social life; he relaxes late at night by jogging. He is also an avid reader, and he delights in listening to music—"I love everything from old Cuban danzónes to modern new wave music," he remarked.[2] That eclectic choice of music is perhaps a reflection of Longoria's bicultural upbringing.

I was born in Bayamo—a city located in Oriente Province, Cuba—in 1958, and I came to the United States with my family when I was four years old. There is little I remember of my birthplace, and at times it is difficult to separate events I actually witnessed from endless reminiscences repeated by family members. However, I clearly remember the day we left Cuba. My parents, sisters, and I stood on our front lawn and said farewell to many friends. I knew something was wrong but did not comprehend any political implications. We got into a taxi that took us to the airport. I sat in the backseat of the cab and watched the crowd walk to the other side of the street as they waved to us. It was an emotional moment for my family, but my thoughts were filled with the excitement of our forthcoming travels.

Mother remembers our arrival in the United States as a frightening experience. Immigration officials detained Father at the airport because his passport was not in order. Mother and the three of us, ages four, six, and eight, were taken to a shabby hotel on the outskirts of Miami. She did not speak English and could not understand what had occurred. Fortunately, Father rejoined us a few days later. We remained in Miami for a brief period and then moved to New Orleans, where Mother's uncle lived. Incidentally, my great-grandmother, who was German, resided in New Orleans. My great-grandfather was a member of the Cuban consular corps and met her on one of his many travels to the city. They married and return to Cuba.

Our first residence in New Orleans was located in Parkchester Apartments, a housing complex where many Cuban families were lodged when they arrived in the city. Father found employment in various veterinary hospitals, where he cleaned cages and performed similar menial tasks. In Cuba he had worked with large animals as a licensed veterinarian. Eventually he met requirements for accreditation in the United States and currently is a veterinarian and faculty member of Louisiana State University, working with small animals. Mother was a teacher in Cuba prior to her marriage. She studied nursing in the United States and last year retired from a rewarding career as a registered nurse.

I acquired a cursory knowledge of English from watching television programming before I attended school. My sisters were less fortunate, and they were required to repeat a year of schoolwork while they learned English. Still, I encountered problems adjusting to school. Teachers and students were kind to me, but I missed my family and felt alienated whenever I did not understand what had been spoken. Once I mastered English, I enjoyed school and became a good student. While attending undergraduate courses at Loyola University, I decided that my mission in life was to learn public interest law and work with the Hispanic community and the disenfranchised.

Confronted with economic reality when I graduated from law school in 1983, I willingly accepted an offer to join the prestigious firm of Fawer, Brian, Hardy, and Zatzkis. I was involved primarily in litigation of state and federal criminal defense cases, and appellate work, as well as personal injury and tort suits. It was an excellent learning experience, and I remained with the company for three years. But in 1986 I chose to return to my original commitment to aid an underrepresented segment of the community. With Michele Gaudin, I formed the partnership of Gaudin and Longoria. We handle all types of civil, criminal, and administrative cases, including litigation and consultation. At first it was a monetary setback, and I was forced to move back with my parents. However, the outcome proved worthwhile, and I am delighted that over 60 percent of my clientele are Hispanic. Moreover, I am supervising attorney of a clinical project at Tulane Law School. The program was established to work with Cubans who migrated to the United States as part of the Mariel flotilla and are incarcerated as a result of a felony conviction. The project provides legal representation to those who wish to appeal deportation. While [I'm] on the subject of Marielitos imprisoned in Louisiana, I served as mediating attorney at the Cuban prisoner uprising in Oakdale in 1987.

The Hispanic community in New Orleans has great potential but at times is fractionalized. Several civic organizations have emerged promoting political, social, and economics programs that are beneficial to our group. I belong to several of them and feel their efforts and common goals will bring about a unified society. The following comments will briefly describe the work of some of these organizations and my affiliation with them.

I was appointed to Mayor Sidney Barthelemy's Hispanic Advisory Board for the city of New Orleans. The board serves as liaison between city government and services that need to be addressed in the Hispanic community, and to promote voter registration. I am gratified that the mayor has taken cognizance of our group and has formed the board.

On a national level, I was appointed [by former President Ronald Reagan] to the Advisory Committee on Hispanic Population for the 1990 census. The committee reported its findings to the U.S. Department of Commerce. It was an exhilarating experience to attend the hearings and introduce policy that would minimize an undercount of the community.

Locally I serve on the board of two clubs that promote Hispanic culture and social gatherings. Cervantes Fundación Hispanoamericana de Arte is a nonprofit organization that produces plays, concerts, and *zarzuelas* [musical dramas dating to 1657 Spain]. These productions provide audiences with an opportunity to experience Latin American theatrical traditions. During each engagement a special performance is held for Spanish-speaking residents in nursing homes, and transportation is provided for them. The main function of Hispanidad is to commemorate Columbus Day, referred to in Latin America as El Dia de la Raza. Its steering committee, composed of representatives from existing Hispanic clubs, plan workshops, beauty pageants, dances, and a parade.[3]

Professionally, I serve as vice-president of the Hispanic Lawyers Association, a club that promotes voter registration and provides scholarships to Hispanic students who plan to remain in New Orleans. The membership schedules talks on the importance of education at schools containing large Hispanic student enrollment.

Additionally, I serve on the board of the Louisiana Hispanic Chamber of Commerce, a trade organization that promotes Hispanic businesses located in the state and meets with government officials to improve prevailing economic conditions. It sponsors a series of networking programs to make its membership aware of the many services available from Hispanic firms. To foster increased international trade in Louisiana, it has established connections throughout Latin America.

I believe New Orleans is extremely Latin in its life-style and therefore find it perplexing to understand why economic growth with Latin American countries has not occurred in a city with this background. I have relatives in Miami and visit with them frequently. Although it has a large Cuban population and Spanish is spoken throughout the city, it remains basically an American city, with its fast pace and puritan work ethic. Similarly, residents living in other cities throughout the United States appear to live to work. On the other hand, New Orleanians work to live. They will always take time to enjoy their cherished traditions, and that is strictly a Latin trait, whether it be French or Spanish.

Those Hispanics who lived during my parents' generation are to be praised for their many accomplishments. As immigrants, their main goals were to survive and educate their children. They socialized with members of their own nationality and tended to be divisive. My generation grew up exposed to different cultures. As a result, we emphasize similarities among Latin Americans rather than their differences, and we can interact with persons of many nationalities. Our goals include [raising] community consciousness and bringing forth a united community. I am happy that I have been able to serve the community, and I look forward to continuing this work in the future.[4]

5

A CREOLE INSTITUTION—
FOOD

LAGNIAPPE

The Creole cuisine in New Orleans has been evolving since the city's founding in 1718. During its early years it combined elements of French and Spanish food preparation, flavored with herbs sold in the open-air market by native Indians and blended by black cooks. Ingredients used were those readily available in the area. The local custom of leisurely dining in restaurants began during the prosperous era of the 1830s. Business-people and travelers visiting the city enjoyed the savory dishes featured in local establishments and recommended the city cuisine upon their return home.[1]

The recent migration of Hispanics has witnessed the rise of restaurants featuring Latin American dishes. If history is any guide, these dishes will in turn eventually influence and be influenced by the city's Creole cuisine. In the process both will become richer.

NANCY CORTIZAS

When I consider opening a new restaurant, I estimate the capital needed to run the operation. But from past experience, I know it is equally important to decide beforehand how many hours you plan to devote to the restaurant and the type of clientile you wish to attract.

✸

Nancy Cortizas listed these requirements as key components to owning a profitable restaurant. Although her professional training was in education, she prefers operating a restaurant and always gives careful consideration to any new proposals for increasing its profits. She, along with José Cortizas, her husband, owns Liborio Restaurant, well known in the city for its excellent Cuban cuisine. She supervises the waiters, greets customers, and purchases the food; he is the prodigious chef. Both were present during our meeting. Nancy Cortizas provided a spirited narration, while José Cortizas added pleasant commentary.

Nancy was born in Cuba and married José in 1960. A few months later they came to the United States, fleeing political oppression. They lived in Miami for 10 years and in 1970 moved to New Orleans, where José found work as a welder. To supplement their income, they bought a glass-enclosed, drive-in stand where Nancy sold refreshments; called La Caridad, it became the first in a series of successful ventures. Nancy said her husband possesses keen judgment in choosing sites for lucrative operations. To meet his standards, a site must be located in a neighborhood where customers will feel fairly secure when exiting the restaurant, it should be close to commercial property, and it should have ample parking space.

Nancy proudly stated that her two sons were attending college and that, on graduation, her younger son would enter law school, while the older one would become a restaurateur. She spoke excitedly about future plans to expand her take-out service. Because Liborio has enjoyed an outstanding reputation as consistently offering superior Cuban food, she felt that a well-planned advertising program would draw former customers to this service.

I was born in the city of Guantanamo, located in Oriente Province, Cuba. Father was in the military, having enlisted in the army prior to Fulgencio Batista's rise to power. Mother was a homemaker whose ancestors were coffee growers. I was an only child and attended Catholic schools. After completing studies in elementary education, I taught primary school for six years. I met José Cortizas by coincidence, during the Cuban revolution. One day when Mother and I were alone at home, soldiers began firing at our roof. We became frightened, and Mother said she would stop the next soldier who passed by our house and explain to him that we were not enemies but sympathized with their plight. The next soldier who approached our house was José Cortizas. Mother spoke to him while I stood nearby. He enjoyed our company and returned often to visit with us. In time we became good friends and were married on 17 July 1960. A few months later we left our homeland.

My husband came to the United States on a 30-day tourist visa but was not allowed to take money out of the country. When he arrived in Miami, friends directed him to a house where Cubans resided and he spent the night sleeping on their living room floor. The following morning he walked from Miami to Miami Beach searching for a job. Although he did not speak English, he found employment at a hotel. I arrived three months later and found work at Miami Laundry. Although I had difficulty speaking in English, I learned my job quickly and in time handled responsible positions.

On the other hand, Mother had difficulty leaving Cuba because Father could not go with her. Fortunately, the Haitian consul offered to take her with him when he returned to Port-au-Prince. He made arrangements for her to stay at an orphanage sponsored by Madame Duvalier. She enjoyed her stay in Haiti and met new friends, including a Puerto Rican couple who were caretakers at the institution. When she arrived in Miami six months later, we immediately filed a petition for her residency in the United States. Subsequently Mother went to work at Miami Laundry as a seamstress.

Although our combined salaries were adequate, my husband attended welding school to learn a trade. A Cuban friend came to Miami recruiting welders to work for a company located in Louisiana, and he offered my husband a job. José accepted, and in 1968 my older son, Felipe, who was born in Miami in 1961, and I accompanied him to New Orleans. We moved to an apartment in the uptown area of the city. At first I was pleased with my husband's wages but a year later suggested that we should augment his salary with additional income so we could live in comfort. That same evening he suggested that we should buy a drive-in stand, located nearby, where we could sell snowballs and ice cream. We bought the business [Snow Wiz Kitchen], and I managed the refreshment stand with help from a cousin recently arrived from Cuba. At first we sold ice cream and snowballs. Since the facility was equipped with a machine that made doughnuts, my husband learned how to prepare them. He made two batches every day—one early in the morning and the other in the afternoon, before he went to work. After school, children would patronize the stand and buy snowballs, ice cream, and hot doughnuts.

A Honduran friend suggested that we should sell *yuca con chicharrón* because Hondurans living in the area would purchase the food. *Yuca* is a vegetable that has edible rootstocks, and *chicharrón* is fried pork skin. Because this entrée did not enjoy the same degree of popularity in Cuba as it did in Honduras, we had to learn how to prepare it. Our friend taught us how to fix the gravy customarily poured over the meal. However, the first attempts to fry *chicharrónes* proved disastrous when hot grease splattered everywhere. Happily, Mother arrived from Miami and showed us how to fry pork skins. Next we located a food distributor who could provide us with a steady supply of *yuca*, as it was not readily available in local stores. Once we added the meal to our menu, the food stand became an instant success. In 1971 we moved to a nearby location that contained a few tables and chairs. Then in 1975 we moved across the street to spacious quarters. All restaurants bore the name La Caridad and were well known.

Friends suggested that we move our business downtown, and in 1977 we opened Liborio Restaurant in the French Quarter, with José as chef. He learned how to cook by watching his hired help work in the kitchen, and many times he substituted for them when they failed to report to the restaurant. He practiced until he perfected his style of cooking and felt comfortable in this role. I did the food purchasing, Mother and I supervised the waiters, and Felipe was the busboy. We worked between 16 and 19 hours a day. During August business was generally slow in the French Quarter, and we closed for the month and went on vacation.

One of the food distributors I dealt with owned property that included a small restaurant. Since I had repeatedly expressed a desire to run my own business, he informed me when the restaurant was for sale. In 1978 I bought the luncheonette for $2,300 and called it Nancy's Coffee Shop. I painted the dining area and kitchen and bought new tables and chairs. When we started, we sold ordinary sandwiches but gradually increased our choice of entrées. We began by including a Cuban sandwich in our menu. The sandwich originated in the eastern part of Cuba and is made with Cuban bread, which is similar to French bread but is softer in texture. It is filled with slices of pork, ham, Swiss cheese, green pepper, and butter and is toasted. Next I added a steak sandwich similar to the one my husband served at Liborio. Later I added hot meals. Initially we earned between $60 and $80 a day. With the addition of our new menu, we earned over $700 a day. Mother and two waitresses helped me, but we only worked weekdays, from seven in the morning until two in the afternoon. When my husband saw this profitable venture, he closed the restaurant in the French Quarter and opened a similar luncheonette, calling it Nancy's Coffee Shop No. 2. Both businesses remained profitable until Louisiana's economy began to vacillate. Unfortunately, the Louisiana World Exposition held in New Orleans in 1984 did not help our business. Not only was the exposition poorly attended, but those who came to the event ate mainly at restaurants located on the fairgrounds. Eventually we closed both luncheonettes.[1]

In 1987 we opened Liborio, which is currently in operation. It is located in the business district of New Orleans, and consequently we are busiest at lunchtime. However, our dinner trade is lucrative and includes patrons who attend theatrical productions performed at a nearby theater. We work from 11 in the morning until 3 in the afternoon, and in the evening from 6 until 9. Mondays we open for lunch; Saturdays and Sundays we open for dinner. Our menu is diversified and offers a choice of two or three specials daily. We feature Cuban dishes such as *boliche asado* [Cuban-style roast beef], *ropa vieja* [shredded beef with plantains, rice, and beans], Cuban-style fried chicken, and roasted pork.

Recently I started a take-out service involving daily delivery of meals to households. This custom is called *cantina* in Cuba. At present my customers live primarily in the uptown area; they include professors and students associated with Tulane University and local residents. At one time I had as many as 33 customers, and feel that with proper advertising I could expand it to a larger business. My husband does not share my enthusiasm for this service, as he would prefer limiting his work schedule to where he would only serve breakfast and lunch.

I am excited that Felipe will enter the restaurant business. As an enthusiastic young man, he has many innovations that he plans to introduce to the profession. I am proud that both sons are Americans of Hispanic heritage. It was difficult leaving Cuba, because as an only child I enjoyed a life full of prosperity and pleasant surroundings. However, I became an American citizen and have adapted to American customs because the United States opened its doors to me when I was facing imminent political imprisonment. I respect the United States and am content and living well in Louisiana.[2]

BELLA G. TORRES

I observed that even though many Hispanics lived in New Orleans, there were no tortilla factories in the area. So whenever I visited my mother in Dallas, I would return with tortillas, taco shells, and other foods and sell them to my co-workers in New Orleans. Then I got the idea to start my own tortilla factory!

That tortilla factory—El Sol—has now been in business for 19 years, its prosperity a result of Bella Torres's hard work and sense of purpose. For many years she worked 14 hours a day, six days a week. "I suffered many disappointments," she said at our meeting, "because I was a woman who did not have as much business experience as other Americans. But little by little I was able to develop my business." Today 60 restaurants in three southern states use her products regularly, and El Sol remains the only outlet in the area for fresh tortillas and nacho chips.

Torres is friendly, unpretentious, and precise in her conversation yet open to all questions. During our initial interview she suggested that I return the following day to see her factory in operation; the second interview consisted of her commentary on various aspects of producing tortillas on a large scale. Although Torres enjoys talking about El Sol, she is equally at ease conversing about her four children, politics, travel, the United States, and her native Honduras.

I was born in San José de Colinas, a peaceful town in the department [a geographic division] of Santa Bárbara in Honduras. My parents are Salvadora Perdomo and José Garcia Davis. I have 10 brothers and sisters. Some became merchants and mechanics; others studied law. But all of us were involved in the business world for many years, helping Father in the car-battery factory he owns. We moved to San Pedro Sula, a city in northern Honduras. I attended local Catholic schools. I married Oscar Riecken when I was 20, and opened a grocery store. Unfortunately, five years later my husband died in a drowning accident and I was left a widow at 25, with two children.

In 1958 I came to the United States in search of economic opportunities and to educate my children. I chose New Orleans to be near friends and relatives who lived here, and resided near an area called the Irish Channel, where there were a sizable number of Hispanics. [Then] when the federal government subsidized low-cost housing developments in outlying areas, some residents took advantage of their availability and moved to subdivisions such as Holly Heights, which is now populated mainly by Hispanics and is located in Kenner, a nearby city.

Friends helped me find a job at Foster Company, a factory that makes items of heavy canvas material. It was very cumbersome working with this fabric, and I stayed there only a few weeks. Soon afterward I went to work as a seamstress at Deansgate, a company that manufactured men's clothing. Work was tedious, but I remained there 11 years. While working at both places I never experienced discrimination, even though I could not speak English. In fact, co-workers always tried to help me. Because I wanted to be self-employed, I enrolled in the U.S. payroll savings program to save enough money to begin my own business.

In 1971 I opened a tortilla factory with my savings and secured a loan from the U.S. Small Business Administration to purchase equipment. In Los Angeles I brought machinery from Casa Herrera that mass-produced tortillas and visited factories, both in that city as well as in Dallas, to observe daily operational procedures. I started the company with a partner, but in less than a year I was sole proprietor. It was difficult in the beginning, but I learned to operate the business after overcoming many unforeseen problems. However, I received support and assistance from my sister, Leysabel Paz, who supervises the office staff and serves as bookkeeper.

Our facility was located in the Irish Channel, and I opened a small retail store at the factory site. I thought there would be a constant stream of Hispanics who would purchase tortillas, but that was not the case. Hispanics preferred thicker tortillas than those produced by the machine. (As a rule, they make their own tortillas for daily consumption and buy those that are mass produced when they require large quantities for parties.) I approached grocery stores and restaurants to acquaint them with my products. Selling nacho chips and tortillas to retail outlets was difficult, since food manufacturers in Texas and California were also vying for this market. However, Mexican restaurants—who'd previously bought their products from out-of-state suppliers—preferred to buy fresh tortillas locally. My first customers included a fast-food chain and two full-service restaurants. Gradually sales became lucrative, and in a year I was able to buy additional machinery and a small delivery truck.

The process of producing high-quality tortillas and nacho chips depends on the manner in which cornmeal is ground. Only an experienced corn grinder can determine the proper texture of the dough. Every day 5,000 pounds of corn kernels, along with lime and water, are cooked in huge kettles. It takes about an hour to cook the corn. After soaking the corn overnight, it is washed and ground. Later it is pressed into a chute that leads to a conveyer belt where it is first cut, by molds—either as tortillas or nacho chips—and then slowly passes over an oven where it is baked. When the tortillas are cooled, they are packaged in bundles. Ten employees are needed for the entire procedure. Even though I am busy in my office talking to customers and checking orders, I make several trips to the processing area to see that the operation is carried out correctly. Currently we process 100,000 dozen tortillas and 3,000 pounds of nacho chips every week.

Our headquarters are now housed in a large facility on the west bank of New Orleans, in the city of Gretna. There are 16 employees on the payroll, and people of many nationalities and races have worked for me. But because it is easier for me to communicate in Spanish, I now hire mostly Hispanics.

Business continues to grow, even though the local economy has been at a standstill; I guess it is because people still have to eat. Increased tourism to Louisiana has helped me because hotels and convention centers use my products whenever they plan events highlighting Latin American themes.

Each year I sponsor services held at St. Teresa of Avilla Church on the feast day of Our Lady of Guadalupe.[1] Festivities include a *mariachi* mass, which is conducted in Spanish and features Mexican music and folk musicians, followed by a reception with music, refreshments, and presents for children. The event, held on or around 12 December, is well attended, and it is my way to pay the community back for all the benefits I have received.

In 1961 I married a Honduran and had two children. My older daughter is a nurse and lives in Miami; a son has a master's degree and lives in Gretna. My other son is an electronic technician and works for a company that produces soft drinks. And a teenage daughter also lives in Gretna.

I try to keep abreast of political issues, both in the United States and in Honduras. I participate in mayoral campaigns and closely follow international politics. A few years ago I was appointed commercial consul of Honduras. This honorary position was established to encourage greater interest in products available from Honduras, including brooms, plantains, wooden doors and ornaments, and perishable fruits. At the same time, it serves as a referral service for persons interested in starting trade with Honduran companies.

I have lived in the United States over half a lifetime and thus feel at home both in New Orleans and in San Pedro Sula. I appreciate the many awards I have received as a minority businesswoman, especially the citation from Louisiana Governor Edwin Edwards. I look forward to increased business, and future plans include a tamale factory. I feel the United States is still the land of opportunity where all this is possible, even for newcomers.[2]

ANGEL MIRANDA

Many persons in the Anglo community hold the opinion that all Hispanics are alike. As a Spaniard I speak the same language commonly spoken by Central and South Americans, yet I differ from them in other aspects. My interests and traits are comparable to those of Italians and other Europeans.

✳

During our meeting Angel Miranda spoke at length on Spain, referring to its former colonial empire and its lasting influence on New Orleans, and cited upcoming events scheduled in Barcelona and Seville in 1992, year of the Columbian Quincentenary. In this connection Miranda compared the manner in which Spaniards from different regions prepared for these events. As a rule, he said, inhabitants residing in the northern part of Spain were dynamic workers, while those living in the southern region worked at a leisurely pace. As a result, the city of Barcelona was ready to host the 1992 Olympic Games, whereas officials in Seville were behind in their plans to welcome visitors at a forthcoming world's fair. Yet Miranda felt confident Seville would complete all contractual projects prior to the intended opening in 1992.

Beginning in 1981, when Miranda arrived in New Orleans, he frequented España Restaurant, the city's only establishment specializing in Spanish cuisine. When España ceased operation, Miranda decided to open a comparable restaurant, though he lacked prior restaurant experience. Admittedly, he made mistakes in construction plans but fortunately was able to rectify them, and in 1989 he opened Restaurante Altamira. Miranda noted that he patterned the restaurant after bistros commonly found throughout Spain. Since its inception, local columnists have acclaimed the restaurant, endorsing its food, service, and Iberian ambience.[1] Customers include Americans as well as Latin Americans, and dinner reservations are hard to come by on weekends. Angel Miranda is an ambitious young man whose persistence will continue to serve him well in future projects.

I was born 37 years ago in Seville, Spain. Father enjoyed a career in the military, and Mother was a housewife. Father is currently retired from the army and living in Spain; Mother died eight years ago. Seville is a beautiful city that once served as the center of economic activity between Spain and its colonies. As a consequence, the Archivo General de Indias, a facility housing extensive documentation on the Spanish colonial period, is located in the city. Seville is also known for its annual festivities held during Holy Week.

I attended the University of Madrid but did not finish my studies in aeronautical engineering. Instead, in 1979 I signed a three-year contract as sales representative in Venezuela with Representaciones Loncho, a company selling industrial equipment to Latin American countries. At the outset I lived in Caracas and later moved to Carúpano, a small town on the east coast of Venezuela. The third year I transferred to Cumana, a town located between Caracas and Carúpano. Prior to my employment in Venezuela I met and courted Solangel Calix, who came to Madrid to learn flamenco dancing. Solangel was Honduran but for many years had lived in New Orleans with her family. In 1980 I traveled to New Orleans and married Solangel. We returned to Cumana and remained until I completed all contractual obligations.

Due to the depressed economy in Venezuela, we chose to move to New Orleans, where I found employment as a handyman doing general maintenance work. My work included painting and servicing simple repairs. A year later I found comparable work at higher wages in another apartment complex, and I remained there for six years. Meanwhile, Solangel opened a dancing school in Kenner, Louisiana, where she taught flamenco dancing.

When I settled here in 1981, I was impressed by the surrounding Spanish atmosphere, yet was puzzled when New Orleanians referred only to its French colonial occupation. Regardless of that, time spent in Seville allowed me to perceive like conditions in architecture, cuisine, and outdoor revelry existing in both cities. I knew Spanish restaurants existed in the French Quarter during Spanish rule, but by the latter part of the twentieth century there was only one public eating place concentrating on Spanish cuisine and it was located in the suburbs. When España Restaurant closed in 1987, I was determined to provide an area steeped in Spanish tradition with a type of restaurant usually found throughout Spain.

A friend suggested a site in the warehouse district of the city.[2] When I saw the location, I knew I had found a choice neighborhood. Last year I came upon a building for lease that was directly across from the Riverwalk and near the New Orleans Convention Center. Although the location was excellent, the facility was in disarray and had been vacant since the Louisiana World Exhibition held in New Orleans in 1984. I contacted the landlord and spoke to him about my plans and my limited funds. He liked the project and drew up a five-year lease that quoted low rent for the first year. The fee would increase at the start of the second year but thereafter would continue at the same rate for the remainder of the contract.

Acquaintances offered little encouragement. Some said I was crazy; others said I would never obtain a liquor license. Yet I felt confident. Because I thought a liquor license would be difficult to secure, I immediately applied for one. To my amazement, I received the permit the following week. I applied for a loan through Citywide Development Corporation and spent a month completing numerous forms required by the agency. When I phoned to see if my loan had been processed, the gentleman assigned to my application informed me that I had requested an exorbitant amount. Initially I had requested $90,000; now I reduced the request to $45,000. Three weeks later the agency informed me that I needed a cosigner. My mother-in-law, who owns property, agreed to serve as cosigner. Then the agency said that I would have to finance half of the $45,000 through a bank loan. I promptly received a bank loan for $22,500 because I had established good credit rating. When I called Citywide to tell them I had secured a bank loan, an agency spokesperson said they decided not to finance my restaurant. In recalling my initial conversation with a Citywide employee, I remember telling him that I would open a restaurant regardless of whether I got a loan from them. I guess they thought I was foolish to start a business without prior experience. In the end, the bank loan, along with the use of my credit cards, covered the cost of construction and equipment. Relatives living in Spain provided funds to cover initial daily operating costs.

When I opened the restaurant, my first customers included a group of Spaniards who were attending a convention in New Orleans. During their visit they returned to Restaurante Altamira several times and ate, drank, and danced. After their departure my wine cellar was empty, and that was conclusive evidence that I operated a pleasing restaurant. At present the restaurant is running smoothly, and we are covering all expenses.

The facility includes an area for entertainment that may be viewed from any table. Every night we have entertainment. Guitarists perform during the week, and on weekends we have two shows featuring flamenco dancing. (Prior to our entertainment, flamenco dancing had not been exhibited on a regular basis in New Orleans.) Various dance groups perform and occasionally Solangel Calix. My customers include Americans and Latin Americans. As a rule, Americans dine early and attend the first show. On the other hand, Latin Americans dine later and remain for the second performance.

Most restaurateurs are constantly inventing new dishes or changing their entrées. In contrast, we serve traditional Spanish food. It is mild-tasting, because we use few spices. We cook with olive oil, garlic, and saffron and follow family recipes. Our food is distinctive because it is fresh and simple. We carry on the Spanish tradition of serving our customers free *tapas* [small hors d'oeuvres], which may include croquettes or other selections from our appetizer menu. Because Spaniards enjoy eating meat, our entrées are prepared with lamb, chicken, beef, and rabbit. But we include meals prepared with fish, and, of course, we serve paella Valenciana, which is similar to Louisiana's jambalaya. We offer four types of soup, and for dessert we feature strawberries with whipped cream and custard.

Although our reputation has grown through word-of-mouth, I believe it is important to advertise our services. We place commercials on KGLA, the only radio station in the city broadcasting in Spanish, to reach their listening audience. While Latin Americans normally prefer to dine in places serving their native dishes, they enjoy eating Spanish food and participating in the culture of their ancestors. Additionally, I advertise in *Lagniappe,* the amusement supplement of the New Orleans *Times-Picayune,* and in a weekly newspaper, *Gambit.* Food editors of both publications wrote glowing articles on my restaurant.

Unfortunately, I have no time for relaxation. A short time ago the restaurant was open seven days a week; now we close on Sundays. However, many times I come to work on Sundays to complete needed repairs. I am pleased that the establishment is successful. Future goals include opening a restaurant in Seville that will feature New Orleans Creole cooking. I was thrilled when I brought a bit of Spain to New Orleans; now I want to bring a part of New Orleans to Spain. If my plans are put in operation, the restaurant will open in 1992 to coincide with the start of the world's fair in Seville.[3]

6

CONCLUSION

NEW ORLEANS 1991:
THE HISPANIC COMMUNITY

Continued development of small businesses in New Orleans will promote a stable economy.—Sidney J. Barthelemy, mayor of New Orleans

Mayor Barthelemy's statement was included in an interview that covered his administrative plans to revitalize the city's economy.[1] He said revenue derived from small businesses would end past dependency on any one industry.

In keeping with this strategy, the Louisiana Department of Economic Development in 1991 embarked on a new agenda and department reorganization plan entitled "New Directions," key policies of which included (a) cooperative efforts by public and private leadership to bring new industry to Louisiana and (b) an emphasis on developing and nuturing the smaller businesses that provide many of the state's jobs.[2] The plan also called for a Louisiana Development Finance Corporation to work with public and private sectors statewide to develop new business finance programs. MetroVision Partnership Foundation will coordinate such activities for New Orleans and the surrounding parishes.[3]

These programs will provide additional incentives to local Hispanic entrepreneurs whose businesses have heretofore been listed as individual proprietorships rather than corporations. Of the 2,697 Hispanic-owned firms in the state, only 505 have paid employees. The majority of Hispanic-owned firms in Louisiana represent service industries, with retail trade and construction being the next largest areas of concentration.[4] At the same time advertising efforts have stimulated Hispanic entrepreneurs to open agencies geared to serving companies eager to attract Hispanic consumers, whose purchasing power in the United States is now estimated at more than $140 billion.[5] Much research needs to be done on the types of businesses owned by Hispanic entrepreneurs, their length of operation, and their productivity in sales and receipts.

While the state's poor economy has made it a real challenge to maintain a small business in Louisiana, Hispanic businesses have received assistance and direction from trade organizations and government-subsidized agencies. One example is the International Trade Center, organized in 1984 and sponsored by the U.S. Small Business Administration and the Louisiana Department of Economic Development. Among the center's activities are seminars in Spanish on international trade; printed materials and individual counseling on trade and investments are also available in both English and Spanish.[6] Another example is the Louisiana Hispanic Chamber of Commerce which offers similar services to its membership. Its executive officers meet periodically with city and state legislators to discuss major concerns expressed by members and also work closely with other trade organizations and city office holders in promoting commerce with Latin America.[7] And the World Trade Center, in a joint effort with other trade strategists in the city, started "Encuentro," a conference matching international markets with American buyers, suppliers, and manufacturers. Although initially the conference sought only markets in Central America, it later included markets in the Caribbean, Mexico, and South America.[8]

Trade With Latin America

Because cargo handled through ports located on the eastern and western coasts of the United States has increased significantly, officials at the port of New Orleans have been concentrating their efforts on regaining Latin American trade, which has been an integral part of the city's economy for more than two centuries.[9] When the territory became a state, the city of New Orleans, acting as agent for Louisiana, managed and controlled the riverfront. In 1886 the Louisiana legislature passed an act establishing a board of commissioners for the port of New Orleans, charged with regulating commerce and traffic in the harbor and with promoting trade. Later, boat traffic created by companies shipping products to the United States through the port of New Orleans further stimulated trade with Latin America. For example, Vacarro Brothers and Company, which began as an importer of bananas from La Cieba, Honduras, to New Orleans, in 1923 expanded its functions to include passenger service from New Orleans to South American ports and changed its name to Standard Fruit and Steamship Company. Similarly, the United Fruit Company, incorporated in 1899, transported bananas from Central America to the United States through the port of New Orleans. And still another company that strengthened commerce at the port was the Mississippi Shipping Company, started in 1919; under the trade name Delta Lines, the company became a leader in shipping and passenger service between New Orleans and Latin America.[10]

The German naval blockade of ports along the eastern coast of the United States during World War II diverted portions of Latin American cargo to the port of New Orleans by reason of its proximity and greater safety for travel.[11] From 1945 through 1960, trade with Latin America grew, in part owing to the establishment of the International House and the International Trade Mart. The former, sponsored by private industry, opened in 1943 and served as a commercial meeting center for foreign businesspeople; the latter, opened in 1948, offered exhibition and merchandising facilities.[12] In addition, DeLesseps S. Morrison, the city's mayor at that time, encouraged trade with Latin America by creating a municipal department of international relations, with Rafael Urruela, a Latin American, as its first director. Under Morrison's guidance, city officials also joined forces with trade organizations in 1947 to hire Rafael Ordorica, a Mexican, to promote Latin commerce.[13]

Some years later, however, the port experienced a serious decline in its Latin American cargo. Commentators reviewing the reversal cited several reasons. For one thing, poor leadership on the part of trade organizations and the failure of business leaders to establish a well-organized policy toward Latin American businesses apparently caused many exporters to seek contracts elsewhere. For another, massive airport construction in Miami, completed in 1974, transformed that city into a primary airline connection for cargo service with Latin America.[14] Moreover, federal deregulation of the transportation industry now allowed cargo to move faster through alternative modes of transport at lower rates. Deregulation also caused steamship companies to discontinue the practice of including ports along the Gulf of Mexico as routine stops. The aggressive campaigns mounted by other Gulf cities to attract such commerce were a further factor cited for the decline, and here critics asserted that local businesspeople involved with port activities at the time did not plan for adjustments that would restore commercial traffic to the city.[15]

In 1986 the port acquired a new president, who suggested that Latin American and Caribbean markets offered great potential for the city but cautioned that achieving this potential would require a number of years.[16] With this as a goal, port officials in 1989 added a Department of Latin American and Caribbean Affairs to the Division of Marketing and Sales. (Previously, contact with Latin America had been handled through an office in Panama.)[17] The importance of this new emphasis is underscored by a recent U.S. Department of Commerce report indicating that trade with Latin America accounts for 26 percent of the port's world trade by tonnage and 33.8 percent by monetary value.[18] Future growth of the New Orleans port is also vital to Louisiana's economy in general, for the port generates some 47,000 jobs throughout the state.[19]

The creation of a North American Free Trade Zone and a current movement in larger Latin American countries to privatize government-owned companies prompted former Louisiana Governor Buddy Roemer to call for a program through which Louisiana might establish permanent relations with Latin American countries.[20] To this end Roemer met with the presidents of Mexico and Venezuela to discuss mutual problems and to establish goodwill.[21] One outcome of these discussions was the formation in December 1990 of the Pan American Commission, designed to support the state in its bid to become a center for Latin American trade, finance, education, and health care. The governor served as chair of the commission and appointed a vice-chair.[22] Additionally he chose delegates to serve on the following five committees: planning, banking, finance, transportation and medicine.[23] A policy report—prepared for the commission's planning committee and for MetroVision Partnership's Latin American Strategic Initiative Task Force—outlined a unified vision of trade development on a state, regional, and corporate level and called for coordination of informational services to ensure that both businesses and individuals would be well informed when dealing with Latin American countries.[24] To date, the state has opened a trade office in Mexico City and daily air flights have been scheduled between New Orleans and Mexico.[25]

Current Latin American Immigration to New Orleans

Migration from Latin American countries to New Orleans has not ceased. Current arrivals include professionals, others who plan to acquire work skills in the United States, and, of course, some who are in need of direction and assistance. City officials, sympathetic to the newly arrived, have set up a Hispanic Advisory Committee to assess the needs of these new immigrants and have also arranged for immigrant youths' participation in summer programs.[26] In addition, the Latin American Apostolate continues to serve the indigent, providing information on immigration, assistance in translations, and spiritual counseling. The apostolate's employment assistance program has enabled thousands of non-English-speaking people to find jobs, while its other services have supplied food, shelter, and furnishings to those in need.[27] Since 1988 the apostolate has also operated Casa Nicolas, a temporary shelter for homeless young men.[28]

Social workers have expressed concern about a problem facing illegal aliens nationwide. When Public Law 99–603, the Immigration Reform and Control Act of 1986, passed, it contained new standards and regulations for immigration to the United States. Many illegal aliens, believing they satisfied the law's requirements for naturalization, found hope in the new statute, and indeed the legislation did permit many to attain the status of "permanent resident".[29] But the law also contained a clause stating that it was a federal offense to employ or find employment for illegal aliens. Thus, while the ruling has not stopped the flow of young men migrating to this country in search of work to support families in Latin America, it has caused employers to turn them away for fear of prosecution. In this regard are persistent reports that aliens who do find employment are not always paid the agreed-on amount for their labor, since they cannot divulge the injustice to authorities.[30] In any event, thousands of homeless men roam the country in a futile search for work, and studies of this population and of the merits and ramifications of Public Law 99–603 are sorely needed.

Contemporary Hispanic Community in New Orleans

The formation of Hispanic professional clubs to promote opportunities for disadvantaged youths in New Orleans points to growth and maturity among members of the city's Hispanic-American community. In 1989 Spanish-speaking doctors founded the Hispanic-American Medical Association to serve as a center for the exchange of medical information and to mobilize leadership within the community. Each year the association selects four Hispanic high school students interested in pursuing careers in health or politics and sponsors their participation at the National Hispanic Youth Initiative in Health and Policy Development. This annual event, held in Washington, D.C., is intended for low-income students of above-average academic achievement; it provides career counseling and promotes pride in one's Hispanic heritage.[31] Hispanic lawyers too have united, forming the Hispanic Lawyers Association, which counsels potential school dropouts on the importance of education and offers academic scholarships to impoverished Hispanic students.[32] In addition, the Louisiana Hispanic Chamber of Commerce (LHCC) has expanded its focus to include activities aimed at correcting social problems in the area. In this endeavor LHCC board members encourage blue-collar-worker Hispanic parents to learn English, so as to avail themselves of federal programs to aid their families and, perhaps more important, work more closely with their children's teachers to correct potential school problems.[33]

A new type of service organization appeared in 1989 with the establishment of the New Orleans Hispanic Heritage Foundation. Composed of volunteers and supported by city officials and local businesspeople, the foundation has as its sole purpose the planning and producing of Carnaval Latino, a summer event that promotes tourism to the city during the festival and publicizes New Orleans through television coverage shown in the United States and Latin America. While its main attraction is a lengthy musical program featuring local and internationally known Latin American musicians, also enhancing the festivities are Hispanic food, sporting events, and a colorful parade.[34]

The city's Hispanic community has little political unity, and efforts to that end have been mostly sporadic and short-lived. Recently, however, a Hispanic candidate competed for a seat on the city council, and although he did not win the election, his example stirred other Hispanics to run for public office.[35] However, politicians court the Hispanic vote and often attend gatherings sponsored by Hispanic organizations. Prior to his election in November 1991, Governor Edwin Edwards met with LHCC board members and promised the group his full commitment to increase international trade in the state. He vowed to work closely with private industry and Mexican officials to establish Latin American ties and markets and to encourage the growth of international banking in the state.[36]

Past studies and commentaries on the growth of Latin American trade with cities in the United States have pointed to the importance of utilizing the talents of the local Hispanic community in creating this commerce.[37] I hope that as new programs to encourage such trade are developed in Louisiana, state and city officials, as well as leaders in private industry will come to understand that this talent is a rich resource and an important key to program success.

These oral history interviews, while drawing diverse comments from narrators on their reasons for starting a business, nevertheless yielded agreement that the entrepreneurs enjoyed the life-style in New Orleans and that economic opportunities were available to them in the United States.

Research showed the existence of entrepreneurs of Spanish descent in New Orleans during the eighteenth and nineteenth centuries and manifested a continuity to the Hispanic presence in Louisiana since 1769. Newspaper advertisements during this long period disclosed that there were tavern owners, fruit sellers, cigar manufacturers, publishers, hunters, and fishers. These and a host of other economic endeavors pursued by the city's Hispanic entrepreneurs should be further studied.

As a rule, Hispanics living in New Orleans assimilated into the community and became identified as New Orleanians. At the same time, some continued to perpetuate family traditions and kept strong ties with Latin America. Yet the scope of Hispanic influence in the city has been little studied until the recent arrival of large numbers of Hispanics. I trust these voices will encourage historians to reexamine the roles that Spain and Latin America have played in Louisiana history. Indeed, continued documentation of new Hispanic businesses is encouraged to provide insight as future trends occur in the community.

Notes and References

Preface

1. The phrases "Latin American," "Hispanic-American," and "Spanish American" are used interchangeably throughout this volume.

2. Luis Emilio Henao, *The Hispanics in Louisiana* (New Orleans, La.: Latin American Apostolate, 1982), 22–24.

3. U.S. Department of Commerce, Bureau of the Census, *Nosotros = We* (Washington, D.C.: Government Printing Office, [1985]), 5.

4. Joan Treadway, "The Latin Link," New Orleans *Times-Picayune,* six-part series: 13 November 1983, sec. 1, 1, 18–19; 14 November 1983, sec. 1, 1,8; 15 November 1983, sec. 1, 1, 6–7; 16 November 1983, sec. 1, 1,15; 17 November 1983, sec. 1, 1, 12; 18 November 1983, sec. 1, 1, 11.

5. Bruce M. Stave and John F. Sutherland, eds., *Talking about Connecticut: Oral History in the Nutmeg State* (Storrs, Conn.: Connecticut Humanities Council, 1985), 69–79.

6. U.S. Department of Commerce, Bureau of the Census, *Minority-owned Businesses: 1969,* MB-1 (Washington, D.C.: Government Printing Office, 1971), 24–59.

7. U.S. Department of Commerce, Bureau of the Census, *Minority-owned Businesses, Hispanic: 1982,* MB82-2 (Washington, D.C.: Government Printing Office, 1986), 40–80.

8. Octavio Nuiry, interview with author, 22 July 1988.

9. *The 1988–89 Louisiana Business Directory* (Omaha, Nebr.: American Directory Publishing, 1988), 640.

Introduction

1. Greta Nelson Indest, interview with author, 4 February 1982.

2. Much of the information for this historical overview was obtained from the following sources:

Charles L. Dufour, "The People of New Orleans," in *The Past as Prelude: New Orleans, 1718–1968,* ed. Hodding Carter, John W. Lawrence, and Betty Werlein Carter (New Orleans, La.: Tulane University Press, 1968), 33.

Ferdinand Stone, "The Law with a Difference and How It Came About," in *Past as Prelude,* ed. Carter et al., 43–44, 50–51.

C. Russell Reynolds, "Alfonso el Sabio's Laws Survive in the Civil Code of Louisiana," *Louisiana History* 12 (Spring 1971): 137–47.

Edwin Adams Davis, *Louisiana: A Narrative History* (Baton Rouge, La.: Claitor's Book Store, 1965), 104–5, 116–119, 131, 129, 174, 146–151, 202.

Jack D. L. Holmes, *Gayoso: The Life of a Spanish Governor in the Mississippi Valley, 1789–1799* (Baton Rouge: Louisiana State University Press, 1965), 22.

Alcée Fortier, *A History of Louisiana,* vol. 2, *The Spanish Domination and the Cession to the United States, 1769–1803* (New York: Manzi, Joyant, 1904), 9.

Gilbert C. Din, "Proposals and Plans for Colonization in Spanish Louisiana, 1789–1790," *Louisiana History* 11 (Summer 1970): 198.

Mintor Wood, "Life in New Orleans in the Spanish Period," *Louisiana Historical Quarterly* 22 (July 1939): 671, 703, 646.

Walter Prichard, ed., "Some Interesting Glimpses of Louisiana a Century Ago," *Louisiana Historical Quarterly* 24 (January 1941): 43–48.

John P. Dyer, "Education in New Orleans," in *Past as Prelude,* ed. Carter et al., 119.

Alberta Collier, "The Art Scene in New Orleans—Past and Present," in *Past as Prelude,* ed. Carter et al., 147–48.

John Chase, *Frenchmen, Desire, Good Children . . . and Other Streets of New Orleans* (New Orleans, La.: Robert L. Crager, 1949), 204, 66.

Peirce F. Lewis, *New Orleans: The Making of an Urban Landscape* (Cambridge, Mass.: Ballinger, 1976), 36.

Charles Gayarré, *History of Louisiana: The Spanish Domination* (New York: William J. Widdleton, 1866), 622, 105, 312.

Alfred Toledano Wellborn, "The Relations between New Orleans and Latin America, 1810–1822," *Louisiana Historical Quarterly* 22 (July 1939): 711.

3. Orleans Parish School Board, *Annual Report of the New Orleans Public Schools of the Parish of New Orleans, 1920–1921* (New Orleans, La.: E. S. Upton Printing, 1921), 91 insert.

4. Norman Painter, "The Assimilation of Latin Americans in New Orleans, Louisiana" (thesis, Tulane University, 1949), 157.

5. More than half of the women interviewed, who arrived in New Orleans prior to 1959, indicated that they came to the United States in search of economic as well as social independence.

6. Painter, *Assimilation,* 157, 42.

7. Luis Guiterrez, interview with author, 14 December 1986.

8. "Manuel's Tamales: A 58-Year Tradition in the City Keeps up with Trendy Fast-Food Outlets," *City Business,* 24 October 1988, 15–16.

9. Norma Ardon, interview with author, 18 February 1987.

10. Painter, *Assimilation,* 99.

11. Henao, *Hispanics,* 20, 22.

12. Jane Foley, interview with author, 23 February 1988.

13. The Reverend Luis Emilio Henao, interview with author, 9 July 1987.

14. The Reverend Pedro Nuñez, interview with author, 14 March 1987.

15. Angela de Bango, interview with author, 2 July 1987.

16. Henao, *Hispanics,* 22–24.

17. Tom Reilly, "A Spanish-Language Voice of Dissent in Antebellum New Orleans," *Louisiana History* 23 (Fall 1982): 325–33.

18. U.S. Department of Commerce, *Minority-owned Businesses: 1969,* 72, 111.

19. U.S. Department of Commerce, Bureau of the Census, *1970 Census of Population,* vol. 1, *Characteristics of the Population* (Washington, D.C.: Government Printing Office, 1973), pt. 20, Louisiana, table 49.

20. Henao, *Hispanics,* 23.

21. Nuñez, interview.

22. Esperanza Ferretjans Sciortino, interview with author, 23 January 1987.

23. Marinovic, interview.

24. Maria Barreneche, interview with author, 10 November 1987.

25. Maxine Lowy, interview with author, 10 November 1987.

26. Articles of Incorporation of the Greater New Orleans Area Latin American Chamber of Commerce, 10 May 1976, 2, in The Chamber/New Orleans and the River Region Archives, University of New Orleans.

27. U.S. Department of Commerce, Bureau of the Census, *Minority-Owned Businesses: Spanish Origin,* MB72-2 (Washington D.C.: Government Printing Office, 1975), 82, 128; U.S. Department of Commerce, Bureau of the Census, Minority-Owned *Businesses: Spanish Origin,* MB77-2 (Washington, D.C.: Government Printing Office, 1979) 65,100.

28. De Bango, interview.

29. Gloribel Rubio, interview with author, 4 December 1986.

30. U.S. Department of Commerce, Bureau of the Census, *1980 Census of Population,* vol. 1 (Washington, D.C.: Government Printing Office, 1982), pt. B, Louisiana, table 24.

31. De Bango, interview.

32. Almaguer, interview.

33. Nuñez, interview.

34. U.S. Department of Commerce, Bureau of the Census, *1982 Survey of Minority-owned Business Enterprises: Minority-owned Business, Hispanic,* MB2-2 (Washington, D.C.: Government Printing Office, 1986), 54, 123.

35. "Los Hispanos en Louisiana Según el Censo 1990," ([The number of] Hispanics in Louisiana according to the 1990 census *Que Pasa New Orleans,* April 1991, 5.

36. "Analiza: Más Sobre El Censo y Los Hispanos," (Analysis: More About the Census and Hispanics) *Que Pasa New Orleans,* May 1991, 8.

37. U.S. Department of Commerce, Bureau of the Census, *1987 Survey of Minority-owned Business Enterprises: Hispanic Origin,* MB87-2 (Washington, D.C.: Government Printing Office, 1991), 22, 45.

38. U.S. Department of Commerce, *1987 Survey,* A-1, 3.

39. Ruperto Chavarri, interview with author, 31 August 1988.

The Marketplace

1. Davis, *Louisiana,* 134–35, 146.

Amaury Almaguer

1. In May 1990 Almaguer sold his interest in *Que Pasa New Orleans.* In June 1990 he started a bilingual monthly newspaper, *Aqui New Orleans,* similar in content to the magazine and published by Hispanic Marketing Associates.

2. Amaury Almaguer, interview with author, 4 April 1989.

T. Argentina Agurcia

1. Alba Luz de Agurcia, interview with author, 12 January 1987.

2. T. Argentina Agurcia, interview with author, 25 July 1991.

Winston Helling

1. Winston Helling, interview with author, 12 April 1989.

Robert F. de Castro

1. De Castro's reference is to the situation during wartime. According to R. L. Scheina, a historian with the U.S. Coast Guard, "When the German Navy initiated a blocade on the port of New York during World War II, neutral countries, particularly Latin American nations, used the port of New Orleans for commercial cargo. The blocade became ineffective after 1943" (correspondence with author, August 1988).

2. Robert F. de Castro, interview with author, 10 February 1989.

Susan Peñalosa Hurtarte

1. Recipients were bestowed with the Pontalba Award, named after Baroness Michaela Pontalba, daughter of Don Andrés Almonester y Roxas and, as noted in the Introduction, responsible for construction of the first apartment buildings in the United States.

2. By 1969 Tijuana's *Directory of Social Services* listed more than a hundred service agencies (John A. Price, *Tijuana: Urbanization in a Border Culture* [Notre Dame, Ind.: University of Notre Dame Press, 1973], 73).

3. Susana Peñalosa Hurtarte, interviews with author, 16 December 1986 and 16 May 1989.

Ernesto Schweikert III

1. Schweikert is now sole owner of the company.

2. Ernesto Schweikert III, interview with author, 27 August 1991.

José (Pepe) Vasquez

1. José (Pepe) Vasquez, interviews with author, 18 February 1991 and 30 July 1991.

Arts in a Carnival Setting

1. Arthur Burton LaCour and Stuart Omer Landry, *New Orleans Masquerade: Chronicles of Carnival* (New Orleans, La.: Pelican Publishing, 1952), 7–12.

2. Robert Tallant, *New Orleans City Guide* (Boston: Houghton, Mifflin, 1952), 180–81.

George Febres

1. Paul Harvey and J. E. Heseltine, eds., *Oxford Companion to French Literature* (London: Oxford University Press, 1959), 387. Jules Laforgue (1860–87) was born in Montevideo, Uruguay, of French parents but lived most of his life in Paris and wrote in French.

2. Roger Green, "Febres Was Headmaster of Early School," *Lagniappe* (entertainment section of the New Orleans *Times-Picayune*), 14 July 1989, 13.

3. Alejandro Bendaña received a B.A. and an M.A. in history from the University of New Orleans in 1971 and 1973, respectively, and later became the Nicaraguan ambassador to the United Nations.

4. The reference is to Mark Lussier's "The Works of George Febres" (*New Orleans Review* 12, no. 3, Fall 1985, 54–66), an article Febres considered the best explication of his work to date.

5. Brother Michael was canonized as Saint Michael Febres-Cordero on 21 October 1984; Febres went to Rome for the occasion.

6. George Febres, interview with author, 6 March 1989.

Margarita Bergen

1. Bergen received these degrees at, respectively, Bronx Community College, Herbert H. Lehman College of the City University of New York, and City College of New York.

2. Bergen was named "1988 Hispanic Business Woman of the Year" by the Louisiana Hispanic Chamber of Commerce and "1990 Hispanic Woman of the Year" by *Que Pasa New Orleans* magazine; she was also cited as being among the "Best of 1988" by *New Orleans Magazine*.

3. Bergen is also a board member of the French Market Corporation, Christmas in New Orleans, the mayor's International Advisory Council, Carnaval Latino, the French Quarter Business Women's Network, and the Louisiana Hispanic Chamber of Commerce, and The Chamber/New Orleans and the River Region.

4. Margarita Bergen, interview with author, 23 June 1987.

Mario Villa

1. Villa refers here to the Carmen Llewelyn Gallery, located, like his own shop, on Magazine Street in New Orleans.

2. Mario Villa, interview with author, 9 February 1989.

Professionals in the Gateway to the Americas

1. DeLesseps S. Morrison, *Latin American Mission: An Adventure in Hemisphere Diplomacy,* ed. Gerald Frank (New York: Simon & Schuster, 1965), 55–56.

2. Henao, *Hispanics,* 20–21.

Soffy Botero

1. Soffy Botero, interview with author, 13 May 1987.

David Kattan

1. David Kattan, interview with author, 13 March 1991.

Nancy Marinovic

1. Nancy Marinovic, *Hispanics in the City of New Orleans* (N.p. 1985).

2. For more information on these efforts, see "Area Hispanics Can Get Boost from Organization," New Orleans *Times-Picayune,* 14 July 1988, 4A7.

3. Marinovic's activities are profiled in "Nancy Marinovic, Architecture," New Orleans *Times-Picayune,* 3 January 1988, D, 4.

4. The plan is detailed in *Bogalusa Economic Adjustment Strategy: Final Report Prepared for the City of Bogalusa, Louisiana* (New Orleans, La.: Hayden-Billes Associates, in conjunction with Gladstone Associates and F. A. Johnson Associates, 15 December 1979).

5. Nancy Marinovic, interview with author, 16 January 1987.

Salvador Longoria

1. Longoria served as chairperson in 1988.

2. A *danzón* is an Afro-Cuban dance in syncopated rhythm (Nicholas Slonimsky, *Music of Latin America* [New York: Da Capo Press, 1972], 303).

3. Both organizations Longoria cites here were formed by Guillermo de Bango, a former Cuban educator who has worked diligently in promoting a unified community.

4. Salvador Longoria, interview with author, 25 January 1989.

A Creole Institution—Food

1. This information on the cuisine's history is drawn from Tallant, *New Orleans City Guide,* iii, 180–81, and Davis, *Louisiana,* 376–77.

Nancy Cortizas

1. Nancy's Coffee Shop No. 1 closed in 1984; No. 2, in 1986.

2. Nancy Cortizas, interview with author, 17 July 1989.

Bella G. Torres

1. This church was the first in New Orleans to conduct services in Spanish in the 1960s (Nuñez, interview).

2. Bella G. Torres, interviews with author, 28 November 1987 and 29 November 1987.

Angel Miranda

1. Such notices appeared, for example, in *Gambit* (30 May 1989) and the New Orleans *Times-Picayune* supplement *Lagniappe* (18 August 1989).

2. The warehouse district, located near the Mississippi River, was revitalized and warehouses converted to apartment buildings in conjunction with the Louisiana Exposition in 1984.

3. Angel Miranda, interview with author, 28 March 1989.

Conclusion

1. Sidney J. Barthelemy, mayor of New Orleans, interview with author, 4 September 1990.

2. "Economic Plans Would Focus on Small Business," New Orleans *Times-Picayune*, 3 February 1991, D-1.

3. "New Directions a Plum for Roemer," New Orleans *Time-Picayune*, 11 July 1991, D-1.

4. U.S. Department of Commerce, *1987 Survey*, 22.

5. Amaury Almaguer, interview with author, 4 April 1989.

6. Ruperto Chavarri, interview with author, 31 August 1988.

7. Gene Reyes III, interview with author, 11 September 1990.

8. Alejandro Rostan, interview with author, 23 October 1990.

9. Edward McClellan, "Boosting Trade in Our Backyard," *New Orleans City-business*, 9–22 September 1991, supplement A, 23a.

10. Much of this historical overview of the port is drawn from Raymond J. Martinez's *The Story of the River Front at New Orleans* ([New Orleans, La.: Pelican Publishing, 1955], 1–3, 35, 73–81, 83–87, 106–9).

11. Scheina, correspondence.

12. Martinez, *Story*, 60–65.

13. Edward F. Haas, *DeLesseps S. Morrison and the Image of Reform: New Orleans Politics, 1946–1961* (Baton Rouge: Louisiana State University Press, 1974), 64–65.

14. John Levine, *The History of Business Relations between New Orleans and Latin America from 1960–1980,* Special Collections, Tulane University Howard-Tilton Memorial Library, New Orleans, Louisiana, 10–11.

15. Jonathan Maslow, "Trade Blues in the Gulf: The Seaports along the Gulf of Mexico Gambled on Expanding North-South Trade and Lost," *Atlantic,* May 1988, 30.

16. "Latin Climate Better for Port," New Orleans *Times-Picayune,* 24 January 1990, D-1.

17. A. P. Carrerras, interview with author, 23 August 1990.

18. McClellan, "Boosting Trade," 25–26.

19. "Port's Effect on Economy Tops Tourism," New Orleans *Times-Picayune,* 28 June 1989, D-1.

20. John G. Davies, Rolfe H. McCollister, Jr., and Milton J. Womack, *Louisiana—the Pan American Center: A Proposal for Symbiotic Relationships Prepared for Governor Buddy Roemer at His Request* (Baton Rouge: N.p. 1990), 11–12.

21. Transcript of press conference with Governor Roemer regarding the Department of Economic Development and the Pan American Commission, 2 October 1990.

22. "Governor Names New Pan American Commission," *Port of New Orleans Record,* January 1991, 15. John G. Davies was appointed vice-chair of the commission.

23. John G. Davies, interview with author, 2 June 1991.

24. Kristina Ford, Timothy Ryan, Eugene J. Schreiber, and John Michael Webber, *Closing the Business Gap with Latin America: A Strategic Action Plan for Louisiana,* report prepared for the Louisiana Pan American Commission Planning Committee and the MetroVision Latin American Task Force (New Orleans: World Trade Center 1991).

25. "La. Office Opened in Mexico," New Orleans *Times-Picayune,* 21 June 1991, C-1; "Airline Plans N.O.–Mexico Daily Flights," New Orleans *Times-Picayune,* 5 April 1991, C-1.

26. Barthelemy, interview.

27. "Latin American Agency Gave Family a Headstart," New Orleans *Times-Picayune,* 18 February 1990.

28. *Casa Nicolas: Un Hogar Para Jovenes* (Casa Nicolas: A Home For Young People) (New Orleans, La.: Latin American Apostolate, n.d.), 1–4.

29. "Alien Hopes to Slice and Dice His Way to U.S. Citizenship," New Orleans *Times-Picayune,* 22 August 1988, A-1. Nearly 2,000 illegal aliens in the New Orleans area received amnesty.

30. Luis Emilio Henao, telephone conversation with author, 17 September 1990.

31. Mariela Llanos, telephone conversation with author, 9 October 1990.

32. Luis A. Perez, telephone conversation with author, 9 September 1990.

33. Reyes, interview.

34. "Come to the Carnaval," *Lagniappe* (entertainment section of the New Orleans *Times-Picayune*), 21 June 1991, 16–18.

35. "The Candidates: Councilman at Large," New Orleans *Times-Picayune*, 21 January 1991, B-4. Further research on this subject is in order.

36. "The Louisiana Hispanic Chamber of Commerce: Issues-Jobs, Business Growth, Progress!" New Orleans *Times-Picayune*, 16 November 1991, B-2; Gene Reyes III, telephone conversation with author, 18 November 1991.

37. Maslow, "Trade Blues," 30.

Appendix 1

Questionnaire Used in Ongoing Oral History Project with Members of Hispanic Community

1. In what city were you born in [name of native country]?
2. Tell me about your parents and other family members.
3. What schools did you attend in [name of native country]?
4. What did you like the most about your native country?
5. What changes would you like to see occur in your country?
6. Did you work in [name of native country]?
7. When did you decide to come to the United States?
8. What ambitions or goals did you set for your new life in the United States?
9. Did you come to this country alone?
10. Did you travel directly to the United States?
11. Did you find New Orleans similar to [name of native country], or was it difficult to adjust to an entirely new culture?
12. Did you find any similarities in the food, customs, or architecture of your country and New Orleans?
13. Were New Orleanians friendly toward you?
14. Upon arrival, where did you first reside?
15. Why did you move there?
16. Were other Latin Americans particularly helpful to you?
17. Have you experienced any prejudice from native-born co-workers or others because you are Spanish [or because you are a woman]?
18. Tell me about your career and how it evolved.
19. Did you find your job very competitive?
20. Are you interested in American politics?
21. Are you still interested in the politics of [name of native country]?
22. What has been your biggest adjustment made, to date, while living in this country?
23. What has been your most pleasant experience in this country?
24. What do you like about Latin American culture?
25. What would you like to see changed in Latin American culture?
26. What do you like about American culture?
27. What would you like to see changed in American culture?

28. How does the role of the church in [name of native country] compare with the role of the church in the United States?
29. What do you do for relaxation?
30. What is your impression of the Latin American community in New Orleans?
31. Have you noticed many changes in the Latin American community?
32. Do you think that this community will unite politically in the near future?
33. What do you think are this community's most crucial needs?
34. What would you like to see occur in the Latin American community in the future?
35. Now that you have been here for [number] of years, do you feel that you have accomplished your original goals?
36. What is your impression of life in the United States?
37. What would you like to see occur in New Orleans in the future?
38. In closing, what are your personal goals for the future?

Ongoing Oral History Project
Latin American Community in New Orleans
Listing of Participants, 1985–1991

Almaguer, Imara
Almaguer, Amaury
Agurcia, Alba Luz
Agurcia, T. Argentina
Ardon, Norma
Arminana, Tuly
Barreneche, Fernando
Barreneche, Maria
Barthelemy, Sidney J.
Benecomo, Concepción
Bergen, Margarita
Blassini, Ediberto
Botero, Soffy
Buras, Lulu
Bustamente, Norma
Carreras, A. P.
Chavarri, Ruperto

Cortizas, Felipe
Cortizas, José
Cortizas, Nancy
Davies, John
de Bango, Angela
de Castro, Robert
de Cortes, Carmen
de la Fuente, Andre
Febres, George
Fine, Nora
Foley, Jane
Gomez, George
Guiterrez, Louis
Helling, Winston
Henao, Luis E.
Hurtarte, Susana Penalosa
Iglesias, Amalia

Iglesias, Luis
Indest, Greta
Irizarry, Jannette
Jerez, Laura
Jiminez, Norma
Jimenez, Zully
Kattan, David
Kiesling, Blanca
Lampard, Catherine
Lindsey, Lilia
Llewellyn, Carmen
Lombana, Marisol
Lopez, Franklin
Longoria, Salvador
Lovisa, Mario L.
Lowy, Maxine
Lugo, Ernest
McElwee, Hilda
Manzier, Carlos
Marinovic, Nancy
Mayorga, Christian
Menes, Pupi
Miranda, Angel
Molina, Luz Maria
Montenegro, Aurelio
Montenegro, Orlando
Morales, Beatriz
Muller, G. Bill
Murphy, Philip
Nadas, Gina
Napoles, Luz
Nardi, Norberto F.
Nodal, Adolfo
Nuñez, Pedro
Nuriy, Octavio

Olmedo, Miguel
Pedrosa, Betty
Pomar, Juana
Quintanilla, Julio
Reyes, Gene F. III
Reyes, Raul
Reynard, Juan
Ricco, Concepción
Ridley, Joan
Rodriguez, Rafaela
Rodriguez, Rose
Rostran, Alejandro
Rubio, Gloribel
Sanchez, Alfredo
Sampson, Martha
Santos, Nellie
Schweikert, Ernesto
Scortino, Esperanza Ferretjans
Servilla, Delia
Steddon, Ricarda
Stephenson, Maria
Stevens, Myrna
Torres, Bella
Torres, Zoila
Treadway, Joan
Vallejo, Alba
Vasquez, Pepe
Vega, Lourdes
Villa, Mario
Vitrella, Maria de los Angeles
Ward, Maria
Zayas-Pope, Liliam
Zeron, Sandra
Zuniga, Dora

Appendix 2

The following newspaper articles reported information on the entrepreneurs presented in this book. These accounts were first published in the New Orleans Times-Picayune.

A Modest Tribute to the American Dream

Twenty-five years ago, native Honduran Bella G. Torres and her family sold their small grocery store in San Pedro Sula and came to New Orleans looking for work.

She labored 14 years in a suit factory while putting aside a little money from each paycheck to buy U.S. Savings Bonds.

Then about 10 years ago she saw her opportunity. She cashed in her bonds, took out a loan from the U.S. Small Business Administration, and began a tortilla factory on Magazine Street.

"I make tortillas," said Mrs. Torres, abandoning her fluent Spanish for broken English. "I cook the corn, ground the corn, and make the tortilla—fresh tortillas every day."

Today El Sol Inc., which also produces under the "Happy Burrito" label, exports as far as Bermuda and, naturally, supplies selected small restaurants (especially Mexican restaurants) and grocery stores in New Orleans and other areas of Louisiana.

El Sol produces corn and flour tortillas, tostadas and corn chips, and acts as wholesale distributor for Mexican foods it doesn't produce, such as jalapeno cheese and green chillies.

For an immigrant who washed up on American shores with little money and no formal business education ("Nothing. No courses. The business give me experience."), Mrs. Torres is a modest tribute to the classic American dream.

Although she is married and has four children, Mrs. Torres is the sole president and supervisor of her corporation, which employs 12 workers, most of whom are of Spanish descent.

She was the one who targeted the tortilla market in New Orleans, researched it, flew to Dallas, Texas, to absorb operating details of similar factories, and made the final decision to gamble her hard-earned savings.

And it was Mrs. Torres who put in the mandatory 14-hour days in the early years to establish her business as a viable enterprise.

Today Mrs. Torres has trimmed her average work day to about 10 hours. Most of her time is spent in her office, surrounded by telephones ringing with orders, but that doesn't mean she won't be found beside her big vat mixing corn and lime, or on her production line scrutinizing tasty tortillas.

Although she has retained her Honduran citizenship, she says she doesn't want to return to Honduras. "Oh, no," she said. "I like here."

Neither does she intend to wallow in her success—or let sleeping American dreams lie.

According to her sister and secretary, Leysabel Paz, Mrs. Torres recently acquired another loan and more machinery to help meet demand and growing competition from Texas. The machinery is expected to boost tortilla production from 650 dozen corn tortillas per hour to 1,800 per hour—and produce every hour 450 pounds of Happy Burrito corn chips.

"People like chips fresh," Mrs. Torres said. "We make plenty for all Louisiana."

Margaret Fuller
Times-Picayune, 25 July 1982

Frame Company Grows from Sales to Assembly

Robert de Castro loves New Orleans, and to prove it, he plans to spend more than $1 million expanding his picture frame distribution company at the Nashville Avenue wharf.

De Castro had offers to move his 36-year-old company to Kenner to meet his expansion needs, but chose to remain in New Orleans, he said.

The expansion means about 50 more people will have permanent jobs next fall when de Castro gets geared up. Plenty more will get construction work renovating the building he plans to lease at the wharf.

The New Orleans Dock Board approved the lease Wednesday at its meeting. The board controls the property along the Mississippi River in Orleans, Jefferson, and St. Bernard parishes.

The building de Castro wants is now leased from the Dock Board by Jaguar Cars Inc. The car company used the building from 1980 to 1983 to clean its cars before shipping them to its dealers around the country.

De Castro will take over Jaguar's lease of about 7.5 acres of land, including a 100,000 square foot building. His business, Robert F. de Castro Inc., 5357 Leake Ave., currently is housed in a 40,000 square foot building he owns near the Jaguar plant.

De Castro will pick up Jaguar's $68,000 annual lease with the Dock Board until it runs out in 1992. Then he will give back to the board about 20 percent of the land and receive a rent reduction. The board wants to reserve the land for a yard to store and prepare containers for shipment.

With this expansion, de Castro will grow from supplying picture frame parts to assembling and finishing the whole frame. He will get the components, already milled, from Europe.

De Castro said he expects to invent his own special finishes for some of the frames.

De Castro imports all his frame parts through the port at the Nashville and Napolean wharves. He said he did not know yet how much more cargo his expansion would bring the port.

Nan Perales
Times-Picayune, 25 September 1986

Nancy Marinovic, Architecture

Nancy Marinovic will talk as enthusiastically about the Hispanic Chamber of Commerce as she does of her own architectural and engineering firm.

As president of both, her loyalties are not divided, they are multiplied.

She is proud to say that Architectural/Engineering Planning Company, according to the Small Business Administration, is the only one of its kind in the state that is owned and operated by a minority woman. It's a business that started small and now has three architects, three engineers and three planners. "We're not booming, but we're stable," says Marinovic, who is a graduate architect herself.

"My main concern is that there are not too many women going into this type of business. You know, so many women believe it's a man's world, but you can conquer it."

Marinovic, 40, is equally proud of her work with the Hispanic Chamber of Commerce, which was created about four years ago to help not only the Hispanic business community, but to offer assistance to anyone doing business with the community. Today, "we have about 120 members and we are growing every day."

From her own experience, Marinovic says, she knows how Hispanics need guidance when they come to this country."

The Chamber helps those from Spanish-speaking countries with problems such as language, makes suggestions on how to go about getting loans and financing for business, and advises banks to give them a greater understanding of the Hispanic's needs.

Marinovic says the Chamber's future goals are to establish an international trade center for the purpose of exhibiting and selling goods from Latin American countries. "With New Orleans so geographically well-placed for this, it is something that we believe can and and should be done," she says.

A native of Bolivia, Marinovic first came to New Orleans when her father was that country's consul general here. "We went back and forth, but I liked it in New Orleans," she says. "I've put my roots here." She fully intends to stay now that she is married to "a Cajun," David Sutherland. They have a 21-year-old daughter.

Times-Picayune, 3 January 1988

Latin Entrepreneurs Scramble for Business

For the last year, Mario and Susana Hurtarte have been dreaming of goose down and pate.

Their dream is to import pate and other goose products processed by Tres Bon, a company in Mario Hurtarte's native Guatemala, into the United States through the Port of New Orleans.

The Hurtartes' National Enterprises, Inc., a small import-export company in Metairie, would be the distributor.

The Hurtartes are part of a small band of Hispanic business people based in and around New Orleans who, despite currency devaluations, coups and other problems, keep doing business with their homelands.

Nearly 50 New Orleans Hispanic-owned import-export companies do business with Latin America, according to the 1987 Louisiana International Trade Directory, published by the World Trade Center of New Orleans.

The companies, mostly small operations, trade everything from rope to marine paint to agricultural chemicals and fruits and vegetables.

And no one can say it's easy.

Consider the Hurtartes' problems with their goose products.

They've been struggling with Guatemalan and U.S. officials to change import regulations.

The fact is, they say, almost no poultry products of any kind are imported into the U.S. unless they're from Canada, France, the United Kingdom or Hong Kong.

The poultry venture is a new direction for 5-year-old National Enterprises, whose annual sales are $1.5 million. The company's main business is exporting industrial chemicals, electronic equipment and heavy machinery to glass manufacturers, breweries and construction companies in Guatemala, Costa Rica and Panama.

If the Hurtartes can get their business launched successfully, a second leg would include establishing a plant in this country where goose down, used in quilts, parkas and down vests, would be processed. Louisiana would be the Hurtartes' first choice for a plant site.

Octavio Nuiry
Times-Picayune, 3 July 1988

Hispanic Lawyer Helps with Census

When Salvador G. Longoria was growing up in New Orleans, he dreamed of becoming a lawyer, prospering and doing something for society.

The dream was partially fulfilled four months ago when Longoria, the 30-year-old founding partner of Gaudin & Longoria, was appointed to the Advisory Committee on the Hispanic Population for the 1990 Census. The 12-member committee, created by Congress in 1985, is a link between the Hispanic community and the Census Bureau.

"I'm the only appointee from the Gulf South," said Longoria, who began his career in 1980 as a trial lawyer for the New Orleans firm of Fawer, Brian, Hardy and Zatzkis. He specialized in criminal litigation.

"Census figures affect the reapportionment of Congressional seats and federally funded programs," Longoria said. "They are also used by businesses and government agencies all over the country for marketing, planning, zoning and social policy."

The Cuban-born attorney came from a modest economic background in a refugee family. But, determined to excel, Longoria secured an education, partly through academic scholarships.

During the early 1970s, he attended Archbishop Shaw High School in Marrero. Four years later, Loyola University offered him a Breaux Foundation scholarship. After graduating cum laude in 1980, Loyola's Law School awarded him a full scholarship.

His first job was washing animal kennels for his father and uncle, both of whom are veterinarians. But, after a myriad of other jobs, he moved on to work as an attorney.

Over the years, Longoria has served on numerous Hispanic boards, including the Louisiana Hispanic Chamber of Commerce, Hispanic Lawyers Association and the Republican Hispanic Assembly of Louisiana.

"New Orleans is a unique city," he said, referring to the national diversity within the local Spanish-speaking community. "We're not a Mexican-American city. We're not a Cuban-American city. We're a true melting pot."

Octavio Nuiry
Times-Picayune, 2 April 1989

Hispanic Couple Put Hearts into Newspaper

Amaury and Imara Arredondo Almaguer have found success in what they see as the newspaper of the future.

The couple, natives of Cuba and now residents of Metairie, recently began a monthly Hispanic newspaper, Aqui New Orleans than contains articles in English and Spanish.

The result a bilingual medium that Hispanics and Americans can understand and where Americans and Hispanics can find their roots according to the Almaguers.

"We felt there was a need to create a vehicle that would attract the attention of Hispanics in this area, but also of the Anglo community," said Mrs. Almaguer, 36, executive editor of Aqui, the first bilingual newspaper in the state. "We can't live apart from this society so it's up to us to educate those who who don't understand us about what being Hispanic is all about."

Almaguer, 34, is publisher of the Kenner newspaper and remains part owner of the Que Pasa New Orleans, the all Spanish magazine he helped found in 1986: "The Almaguers worked with Que Pasa for more than four years before beginning the newspaper," he said.

They own and operate the newspaper through Hispanic Marketing Associates, which handles public relations and advertising for businesses in the area. The two see the bilingual newspaper as a step ahead of its time, reaching the growing younger generations of Hispanics fluent in both languages.

"Aqui literally means here or here we are," Mrs. Almaguer said because the couple believe it is appropriate for the Hispanic community in the metropolitan area.

"We thought it was perfect. After all, Hispanics in the community are here to stay. We are not going to go away and people have to understand that," she said.

The Almaguers and the Hispanic community in New Orleans is different from others around the country. Of the various Hispanic groups, Cubans are the majority in Miami, Mexicans in Texas and California, and Puerto Ricans in New York. In New Orleans, however, Hondurans make up the largest portion of Hispanics but Cubans are the most active politically and economically.

"In New Orleans the level of educated Hispanics is much higher than those around the country," Mrs. Almaguer said. "There are more professionals, doctors, lawyers. These people speak both languages well and would be completely bored if all the articles were in both languages. So, we have some articles in Spanish, others in English. This way they don't get bored and can practice both languages."

The paper is distributed in the metropolitan area, Morgan City, Baton Rouge and New Iberia, in supermarkets, restaurants, offices, universities, department stores, and wholesale outlets," Almaguer said.

Advertisements are written in both languages so businesses can reach both markets. The Almaguers are working on the third issue, targeted at education in the state, Mrs. Almaguer said.

The response from the community has been overwhelming, she said, with American and Hispanics advertisers eager to be part of Aqui. The paper has grown from 20 pages in its first issue to about 38 in its third month.

"We wanted American businessmen to know Hispanics are doing positive things for the city, the state and the local economy. Mrs. Almaguer said, "Hispanics bring so much to this area and they should be noticed. We wanted to give credit where credit is due."

Almaguer, a former political prisoner in Cuba, came to the United States about 10 years ago. He was one of five political activists who were shot and arrested while demonstrating against Fidel Castro's policies. Three of them died, and Almaguer recovered from his wounds and spent five years in a Cuban prison before being shipped to Spain. He entered the United States in 1980 about a month before the Mariel exiles.

"I feel like I'm still an activist with this paper," he said. "But now I'm an activist for some thing, not against it I want to push people to notice Hispanics, to work with us."

Mrs. Almaguer has lived in the United States for almost 20 years and has a bachelor's degree in Spanish from the University of New Orleans. She is the editorial force behind Aqui, while Almaguer handles production and advertising.

The Almaguers plan to make the newspaper semimonthly. The paper's circulation is about 20,000 and it is expected to be at 30,000 by January 1991.

"We want to help Hispanics integrate into the mainstream of this society and not pushed to the side," Mrs. Almaguer said, her eyes full of emotion. "We want to be a part of that. That will make us happy."

Alina Hernandez
Times-Picayune, 29 July 1990

Powerful Messages from the Visionary Imagists

Visionary Imagism, in the event that somebody hasn't heard, is a regional movement that in recent years has arisen from the abundance of artistic activity in Louisiana. Identified by New Orleans critic D. Eric Bookhardt, Visionary Imagism describes works by a group of mid-career artists whose paintings and sculptures share obvious formal properties and express common concerns.

All of the artists work in a tight, polished figurative style, usually with a palette of jewel-bright colors. All express mystical sensibilities, usually related to topical issues and ideals. Moral concerns often are cloaked in absurdist humor.

The Contemporary Arts Center has mounted a major exhibition of works by seven Visionary Imagists—Andrew Bascle, Jacqueline Bishop, Charles Blank, Douglas Bourgeois, George Febres, Ann Hornback and Dona Lief. The exhibit is an illuminating and long-overdue assemblage of the Visionary Imagists' works, culled from private collections and other sources.

In the exhibit we find clear proof of the existence and significance of the movement. We also discover the strengths and weaknesses of the individual artists.

Works by Febres, in many respects the movement's progenitor, are exhibited appropriately in the center of the CAC's spacious new Lupin Gallery. A native of Ecuador, Febres is known for giving literal, pictorial expression to English-language figures of speech in constructions and drawings marked by fastidious draftsmanship. As owner/director of the now-defunct Galerie Jules Laforgue during the early '80s, Febres represented—and demanded his own high standards from—other artists in the current show.

Bascle uses scrap materials such as string, wire, nylon stockings and metal cans to create witty sculptures that are shaped by the materials' physical properties, and that express primal, universal emotional states. "I want to speak to everybody," the artist has said, "whether they live on St. Charles Avenue, in Lakeview or down the bayou."

Bishop's meticulous paintings and constructions address ecological and re-lated political issues, in a chromatically bright and storybooklike miniaturist's style. A series of paintings she executed two years ago, "Small Mercies," cat-alogs the then-threatened tropical birds that, in some cases, are today extinct. For Bishop, affinities between Louisiana's lush natural environment and that of many Caribbean and Latin American nations provide a springboard for statements as global as Bascle's.

Blank, the most subjective and enigmatic of the Visionary Imagists, paints landscapes and interiors filled with flattened figures that are partially bloated, twisted or shriveled, or that are missing body parts. Often, his figures appear to be undergoing strange metamorphoses. Often too, mysterious lines sur-round the distorted figures, signaling their relation to what Blank calls "things that go on outside that we really don't know about."

Bourgeois, the most conventionally spiritual of the Visionary Imagists, equates the lives of saints with those of music and movie stars. "Both," he has said, "are searching for some higher kind of satisfaction . . . a way to transcend ordinariness." His impeccable paintings and shadowboxlike con-structions portray luminaries such as Aretha Franklin and Elvis Presley, as well as more obscure (if anatomically perfect) mortals achieving transcen-dence. Often the latter are being healed by beneficent nature.

Hornback's gouache paintings and relief constructions are visual puns that, like those of Febre, illustrate everyday figures of speech. However, while Febres models his subjects masterfully to suggest volume and depth, Horn-back deliberately simplifies subjects into flat color areas, surrounded by thin dark lines. More important, Hornback's art—unlike Febres'—concerns the history of manners, particularly as they create special problems for women. "The absurdity of high society in New Orleans," she says, "certainly has in-fluenced my art."

Lief, who grew up in New Mexico, brings to New Orleans her childhood memories of native American life, particularly rituals, and of the testing of atomic bombs. Many of her diminutive ceramic sculptures are shrinelike shadowboxes containing altars, sacrificial steers, skulls, double-headed axes and nuclear devices. In these works, Lief contrasts ancient and modern man's methods of overpowering life-threatening forces. The message of her initially macabre-looking art is that modern man needs to reforge his lost spiritual ties to nature.

Seen as a group, the artists' creations demonstrate enough affinities to ar-gue persuasively that Visionary Imagism is a viable movement or school. Its defining properties are best understood in relation to a earlier regional move-ment, Chicago Imagism, which inspired many of the Louisiana artists, at least by example.

The Chicago Imagists, among them Ed Paschke, Jim Nutt, Karl Wirsum and Roger Brown, began to attract attention in the early '70s. Riveting

131

colors and distortions derived from vernacular sources—tattoos, neon sign-age and pinball machines—characterize Chicago Imagism, a free-wheeling but tough and sleazy manifestation of urban sensibility.

By contrast, Visionary Imagism is lyrical and, above all, spiritual. Its visionary quality might partly be explained by New Orleans' adaptation of Haitian voodoo rites, and by its predominantly Roman Catholic population. Significantly, most of the artists in the exhibit were reared in the Catholic church.

Concern about moral and social ills—a clear expression of spiritualism—also characterizes Visionary Imagism, along with laborious miniaturist technique. Most of the artists manifest apprehension about environmental ill health—and not just with imagery. By working with found materials, Bascle recycles them. By mounting her paintings in second-hand frames Bishop does the same.

The strongest works in the show are those by the most accomplished and subtle draftsmen. Febres has the advantage in this respect, as do Bourgeois, Bishop and Bascle. The exhibit includes works executed over a period of about 10 years. The most recent works document marked technical refinement—and by extension transcendence.

Kudos to the CAC's Lew Thomas for organizing the exhibit, and to Book-hardt for penning an illuminating catalog essay. The exhibit, which will travel, shows that the visual arts are not just alive but flourishing in Louisiana.

Roger Green
Times-Picayune, 4 January 1991

Touching on Greece, Rome

Because cosmetic surgeons and their patients are concerned with aesthetics, it follows that the physical settings in which cosmetic surgery is discussed and performed should look as good as the final product.

And because the aesthetic ideals underlying most cosmetic surgery come from classical antiquity, cosmetic surgeons' offices and waiting, examination and even operating rooms logically should evoke ancient Greece and Rome.

And that's how the Ochsner Clinic renovated its Center for Cosmetic Surgery.

Many hospitals claim to have decorated specialized departments—particularly maternity wards—with an eye to eliminating clinical sterility. But many such design schemes amount to little more than skimpy bandages, haphazardly applied.

By contrast, Ochsner's new Center for Cosmetic Surgery, a project of New Orleans designer Mario Villa, is sumptuous and elegant throughout. Classicized furnishings and building parts combine with contemporary artworks and faux-marbled surfaces to create an imaginative and glitteringly integrated renovation.

The center occupies both sides of a long central corridor on the fifth floor of the Ochsner Clinic on Jefferson Highway in Jefferson. To the right are a reception and waiting room, followed by an examination room, an information office and three doctors' offices.

To the left are two more examination rooms, an open nurses' station and two operating rooms. The entire center encompasses 2,700 square feet.

The reception and waiting rooms immediately announce the stylized opulence of the spaces beyond. The neo-classical note is struck by Villa's slightly tongue-in-cheek furnishings, including—in the reception area—a folding metal screen with inset marble panels and dancing figures.

The reception area also includes two torchieres imitating ancient funerary lamps, flanking a relief sculpture consisting of swagged fabric, which has been dipped in plaster. The spacious waiting room evokes antiquity with an imposing wooden cabinet, the columned front of which re-creates an imagined "Temple of Knowledge."

Perhaps the most dramatic feature of the renovated center is its long central hall. While an immovable "given" in Villa's design, the hall continues the quintessentially classic device for ordering interior space—think of beaux arts museums and Greek revival homes. At the center, classical embellishments also focus attention to the hall's Greek and Roman roots.

Segmented arches veneered with bleached maple and gleaming marble line the hall, suggesting a classical colonnade. At the end of the hall—its dramatic focal point—is an 18th-century, neo-Greek urn, displayed on a lofty pedestal and indirectly illuminated by hidden lights.

The hall is further enhanced by Villa's treatment of the doors leading to the offices, examination and operating rooms. The doors are decorated with rectangular and triangular wooden panels, some marbleized, others fitted together so that juxtaposed wood grains create starburst designs.

Despite their impression of richness, the doors were relatively inexpensive to fabricate. Underneath the decorative panels, the doors are $50 plywood doors, Villa said. Their "bronze" knobs are aluminum knobs plated with bronze.

Decorative devices used in the hall, reception and waiting rooms are repeated in the center's remaining spaces. Lamps, mirrors, tables and other furniture items by Villa continue the center's slightly stagy but humanizing neo-classicism.

Expanses of faux marbling by Don Price have the same effect. Particularly noteworthy is the appearance of Price's marbling in unlikely places, such as the cabinets in the nurses' station, examination and operating rooms.

The doctors' offices were decorated according to each doctor's tastes. Easily the most effective office, combining Villa's furniture with a mirrored wall, is occupied by the center's director, Dr. John Finley.

Finley, a Sunday painter, also contributed a number of his abstract paintings to the center.

These complement canvases by Ann Harding, Pam Moise, and Linda Dantrel, and a small white sculpture of a winged horse by Arthur Kern.

Others who contributed to the center are architect Jim Lynch of Kessels-Dibol-Kessels and lighting designer Ron Katz of Artimide. These and other contributors' efforts are best appreciated when the renovated Center for Cosmetic Surgery is compared to the conspicuously unrenovated Center for Plastic Reconstruction next door.

The Center for Plastic Reconstruction shows what the Center for Cosmetic Surgery looked like: fussy, busy, impersonal and lacking noticeable aesthetics of any kind. Luckily, it will be renovated under Villa's direction next year.

Roger Green
Times-Picayune, 19 January 1991

Miss Margarita's Way

"Saturday night? No, no, no, no, no, darling! God, I have nine or 10 parties to go to that night!" Margarita Bergen was on the phone, declining an invitation, accepting her date book from a secretary and riffling through its pages. In addition to owning and operating the Bergen Gallery on Royal Street, she just may be the city's most visible party girl.

"I'll hire a limousine, not because it's glamorous, darling, it's because I don't like to say no to people, I want to be everywhere, so a car must be there to whisk me away like a politician."

The previous evening, Bergen had been spotted at a benefit function in a bright, cherry-red dress with hat to match. She couldn't stay, she explained, because she was en route to her stand-up comedy class at UNO.

"I open my mouth and people crack down," Bergen explained blithely. "But I want to find out *why* I'm funny."

Originally from the Dominican Republic, Bergen has a command of English that often results in Carmen Miranda-like malapropisms. One of her employees recalls her asking a friend, "Who have you been up to lately?"

But why all the partying?

"It's not just partying to be partying," Bergen insists. "Yes, it is a way of socializing and I am Latin, I always like to have a party going on around me. But some of it is charity, good causes. Some of it is tied to business, openings of artists I know. Every party I go to has a motive, a meaning to me.

"I'm also curious, I like new ideas about how people entertain. How is their food? Sometimes it astonishes me at parties where you expect real chefs and they are serving Popeyes!"

"I like to think I am a good guest, too. I don't want to be bored and people know with Margarita they will never be bored because I'm here, I smile, I laugh, I joke, they see my clothes and hat and you remember it if I'm wearing it!—then I'm off to the next party!

"I'm not a socialite, per se. I'm a businesswoman, but an artist at transforming myself. I have lots of clothes and *everything* matches. I had all my hair chopped off, because I wear hats, so why should I spend two hours and $80 having my hair done? So when I go out, all I have to do is put the hat on my head.

"People always have the wrong impression of me, it's amazing. You said, 'Margarita, you look so pretty last night!' Darling, I wasn't dressed up, I was dressing down! Those were my work clothes!"

David Cuthbert
Times-Picayune, 13 October 1991

Index

The Author

Beatrice Rodriguez Owsley is a certified archivist who currently works in the Archives and Manuscripts/Special Collections Department of the Earl K. Long Library at the University of New Orleans. A member of various professional organizations, including the Academy of Certified Archivists, the Association of American Archivists, the Oral History Association, the Latin American Studies Association, and the Society of Southwest Archivists, she at present serves as secretary/treasurer of the UNO Hispanic Caucus. Her interest in oral history has led to the publication of articles, presentation of papers at professional meetings, and production of broadcasts for local public radio stations in connection with her interviews. She is involved in two ongoing oral history projects: one with retired teachers and administrators associated with the Orleans Parish School Board and the other with Hispanics in New Orleans. She is married, has three sons, and lives in New Orleans.